I0806636

Wendy Murray

Inner Healing the Franciscan Way

A Holy Re-Ordering of the Soul

San Damiano Books
PARACLETE PRESS

2025 First Printing

Inner Healing the Franciscan Way: A Holy Re-Ordering of the Soul

ISBN 978-1-64060-974-7

Copyright © 2025 by Wendy Murray

Unless otherwise noted, Scripture quotations are taken from the COMMON ENGLISH BIBLE. © Copyright 2011. COMMON ENGLISH BIBLE. All rights reserved. Used by permission. (www.CommonEnglishBible.com).

Scripture quotations marked KJV are taken from the King James Version of the Bible.

Scripture quotations marked NIV are taken from the Holy Bible, New International Version®, NIV®. Copyright © 1973, 1978, 1984, 2011 by Biblica, Inc.™ Used by permission of Zondervan. All rights reserved worldwide. www.zondervan.com The "NIV" and "New International Version" are trademarks registered in the United States Patent and Trademark Office by Biblica, Inc.®

Scripture quotations marked NRSVue are taken from the New Revised Standard Version Updated Edition. Copyright © 2021 National Council of Churches of Christ in the United States of America. Used by permission. All rights reserved worldwide.

The San Damiano Books name and logo are trademarks of Paraclete Press.

Library of Congress LCCN number 2025016762

10 9 8 7 6 5 4 3 2 1

All rights reserved. No portion of this book may be reproduced, stored in an electronic retrieval system, or transmitted in any form or by any means—electronic, mechanical, photocopy, recording, or any other—except for brief quotations in printed reviews, without the prior permission of the publisher.

Published by Paraclete Press
Brewster, Massachusetts
www.paracletepress.com

Printed in the United States of America

Praise for *Inner Healing the Franciscan Way*

With this volume, Wendy Murray expresses the heart and mind of the great saint to aid us in our Christian living today. I was led smoothly from life to vows but was grabbed by the insights of "simplicity" as a virtue to cultivate. This is going to be my new "special gift" to give to relatives and new friends.
—**Scott W. Sunquist,** President, Gordon-Conwell Theological Seminary and author of several books, including *The Shape of Christian History: Continuity and Diversity in the Global Church*

In *Inner Healing the Franciscan Way*, Wendy Murray blends a lucid understanding of history, theology, and Scripture with threads of a compelling personal narrative to form a book that is as captivating as it is enriching. I've long been tutored by Murray's journalistic work, but in the pages of this book I was challenged to walk in the way of St. Francis in our time.
—**Jeff Crosby**, author of *The Language of the Soul* and *World of Wonders*

Wendy Murray, in this insightful book, demonstrates how *Inner Healing the Franciscan Way* can infuse into our souls a clear and holy path during our own personal sorrows and victories of the spirit. This is a book that matches the wisdom of St. Francis with a contemporary writer's personal revelations.
—**Christopher de Vinck**, author of *Things That Matter Most: Essays on Home, Friendship, and Love*

In *Inner Healing the Franciscan Way*, Wendy Murray insightfully notes the masculine (Francis) and feminine dimensions (Clare) of the Franciscan vision of life and how they found her after a painful period in her life. This wonderful book highlights the perennial practical wisdom of thirteenth-century Franciscan spirituality that helps re-order the soul in the twenty-first century.
—**Albert Haase, OFM,** author of *The Persistent God: A Guide to Deepening Prayer*

In *Inner Healing the Franciscan Way*, Wendy Murray shares a life-changing discovery: You don't have to be a vowed religious—or even Catholic—to appreciate the sheltering constraints of poverty, chastity, and obedience, or to recognize the uplifting power of humility, charity, simplicity, and wisdom. Murray unpacks the thirteenth-century wisdom that met her in a place of despair and set her on a

path of healing. Contemporary seekers bereft of consolation may draw hope and guidance from this inspiring witness to the transformative practice of Franciscan spirituality.
—**Christine Marie Eberle,** author of *Finding God Along the Way: Wisdom from the Ignatian Camino for Life at Home*

Accessibly written, this book connects ancient and modern thinkers, clarifying Franciscan theology and practice. I especially loved the way the author leads us through the Canticle of the Creatures in ways that help us understand how simplicity and profundity go hand in hand. This book will speak especially to the broken and the lost.
—**Keren Dibbens-Wyatt,** Christian contemplative and author of *Recital of Love*

That Wendy Murray wrote *Inner Healing the Franciscan Way* "as one whose life and belief system were shipwrecked and who found an improbable rescue through an endearing saint," speaks to how the faith, the wisdom, and the practices of St. Francis and St. Clare have continued to shape and save pilgrims through the centuries.
—**Caryn Rivadeneira**, author of *Saints of Feather and Fang*

As I read Wendy Murray's *Inner Healing the Franciscan Way*, I found myself longing to be free from the myriad distractions and ambitions that cloud my vision and keep me from being close to the God I profess to love. I found in this book practical and meaningful ways to apply Franciscan vows and virtues to my very modern life. I highly recommend *Inner Healing the Franciscan Way*.
—**Fernando Ortega**, acclaimed singer-songwriter of Christian music

With lyrical prose and deep transparency, Wendy Murray intertwines the lives of St. Francis and St. Clare with her own journey of recovery from searing heartbreak. The result is an engaging read, with much to ponder.
—**Gwenfair Walters Adams, PhD,** Professor of Church History and Spiritual Formation at Gordon-Conwell Theological Seminary

TO KATE

Where swaddled in strips
Of a torn shirt
Just as an angel told
He shines in the dark valley
—Anne Porter

ALSO BY WENDY MURRAY

Clare of Assisi, Gentle Warrior (2020)

A Mended and Broken Heart,
The Life and Love of Francis of Assisi (2008)

On Broken Legs (2004)

Facing Forward (2002)

Sacred Journeys (2002)

Day of Reckoning (2001)

The Warrior King (2010)

CONTENTS

Inner Healing the Franciscan Way

We have been called to heal wounds,
to unite what has fallen apart,
and to bring home those who have lost their way.
—St. Francis

INTRODUCTION

I will make the blind walk a road they don't know,
and I will guide them in paths they don't know.
But I will make darkness before them into light
and rough places into level ground.
These things I will do;
I won't abandon them.
—Isaiah 42:16

It took the wreckage of my life to bring me to the place where I could see—if achingly—the healing and empowering force of Franciscan vows and virtues. It took losing all that had once defined my life—my role as a wife, my profession as a national journalist, my intimacies and my income, the power of my station, and the associated losses and humiliations. All of it. Mine was a ruined soul.

The following pages explore new themes about spiritual rehabilitation which came to me through such struggles. I write not to elevate my story (this is not about me) but to lay bare the level of human desolation I confronted in a way that might offer hope for others whose lives, for whatever reasons, have similarly collapsed. The point is, that collapse—any collapse—isn't the end of your story, though it may feel that way. It is the beginning of a new story.

As I ponder the landscape of our times, I am seeing an ocean of seeking, damaged, and ruined souls who seem as lost as I once was, striving and asserting a form of human will in the effort to save themselves, even while nearly collapsing under the weight of so lonely an enterprise. Through it all, over time, I found the healing and empowering force of the Franciscan Way of life. I came to understand it through embodying Francis's own vision for his movement as expressed in the vows and virtues. The model that St. Francis forged for his (then) new and innovative Order lends graces that remain operative for hungry and searching souls even today.

My friend the late Fred Buechner wrote once, "It slays us all, they call it life." And, while the sentiments I impart here arise from a place of hope for those whom life has "slain," it is my prayer that these explorations will scratch out a path toward healing and renewal for any who long for the sacred journey toward higher holy allegiances. It is for those who dare to believe there is hope, even and especially for a ruined life. What follows in these pages is an exploration as to how all aspects of our human experience can be consecrated—the physical, the emotional, the psychological, the spiritual, the material, even the sexual. Each, in its turn, can be refashioned under a new and holy re-ordering. Then it can be said truly, "Don't you know that . . . you don't belong to yourselves? You have been bought and paid for, so honor God with your body."[1]

Who Are the Franciscans?

The Franciscan Order, named for its founder, Francis of Assisi (1182–1226), showed itself at its inception as a rag-tag band of men and women wearing simple earthy tunics tied with a three-knotted rope dangling from the waist and with tonsured hair (see the Glossary). Francis envisioned his brothers as a fellowship of the knights of the Round Table who were called to live a life of chivalry in the hermit's garb of penance. This picture evolved even during Francis's own lifetime. And over subsequent years, decades, and centuries, the Order experienced internal splintering and realignment. By the sixteenth century the three branches of Franciscanism were fully defined and operating in their respective spheres.[2] These branches included the Friars Minor Observants (brown tunic), currently the second largest Order in the Roman Catholic Church, second only to the Jesuits; the Friars Minor Capuchin (brown tunic, often with long beards), the fourth largest; and the Friars Minor Conventuals[3] (gray or black tunic), the branch that most rigorously encourages education and the building of universities. The Order also includes women, as initiated by Clare herself, known as the Poor Clares or "the Second Order," as well as the Third Order (tertiaries), comprised of lay men and women. It is worth noting that the Franciscans have more canonized and beatified saints than members of any other Catholic Order.

The signature feature of the Franciscans when Francis initiated the Order was their threefold vows of poverty, chastity, and obedience. For Francis, these vows represented the imposition of outward constraints that functioned as a wedge to halt the grinding gears of habits of mind and body that lead to self-destruction. He imposed them upon himself, first and foremost, and in turn, seeing the transformative power such constraints brought to his new life and spiritual vision, implemented them as a requirement for those who would similarly assume the rustic tunic.

Francis further exalted the virtues, of which he said, "You most holy Virtues . . . each [of you] puts to rout vices and sins." In contrast to the vows, which impose constraints from the top down, the virtues represent an ascent from the bowels of human reckoning to an inward and upward striving toward holiness. The result of these operations in tandem on the human soul—the constraints of the vows and the ascent of the virtues—is the healing of lives. And not healing only, but consecration. Holiness can rise from the last desperate and cynical corners of a shipwrecked life. There is hope, in other words. And the following chapters explore both the vows and the virtues and their respective pathways to healing and holiness.

The Destiny of the Seed

Such healing is written into the code of the universe, as I came to understand in my work as a flower farmer. Simply plant a seed and you will see it. You will understand that a new, perfect, wondrous life is the destiny of those minuscule seeds, mere flecks of dust, that have been cast off, buried in the ground, and trodden under foot. This is the story of every seed. The miracle of the seed is that the very trodding of it, its death and burial, is the portal into its realizing its destiny—it is destined to become a perfect, unique, and fully formed flower.

Yours is the destiny of the seed. You yourself will become that flower. When (and only when) the seed of your life is buried in its rightful place, surrendered to the invisible forces that break through the decay, God does something altogether original with the fragments. I assure you, the exercise of the vows and virtues will get you there.

When I've considered my desire to extol the graces of Franciscan spirituality, I've been compelled to ponder the vows of poverty, chastity, and obedience—vows Francis required of those who would join his Order. I ask myself: How could this form of devotion appeal in any way to a religious seeker? As I've studied at great length the lives of both St. Francis and St. Clare, I've found it self-evident that "Franciscanism" as a concept is wider and deeper than those signature threefold vows. Therefore, the Franciscan Way is accessible and even desirable to anyone, regardless of worldly station or Christian identity. Francis himself realized this when his movement was spreading. Many desired to live in the way of his devotion but had already given themselves in marriage and secular vocation. What was to become of those pilgrims who longed to live the Franciscan Way but whose circumstances disallowed it? Rather than eschew these earnest seekers, Francis answered their cry by establishing what he called "Third Order" Franciscans, or tertiaries, comprised of both lay men and lay women.[4]

The origin of the Third Order arose as a result of a season of prayer Francis undertook late in his life when he questioned whether he should withdraw from active ministry and retreat to a cave as a contemplative. He solicited the advice of a few of his closest companions, including Brother Masseo and Clare:

> . . . [H]e called Brother Masseo into the woods, and, baring his head, crossing his hands and kneeling he asked: "What does our Lord Jesus Christ wish me to do?" Brother Masseo answered that the blessed Christ's answer to Brother Sylvester and to Sister Clare and her companion was the same: "He wants you to go out preaching, because God did not call you only for yourself, but also for the salvation of others." Then the hand of the Lord came over Saint Francis. In a fervor of spirit he rose up completely on fire with the power of the Most High, and said: "In the name of the Lord, let's go!" . . . From that time on he thought about making a Third Order for the salvation of everyone everywhere.[5]

Francis accommodated the longings of those dear secular people who desired to follow his way, but whose circumstances mitigated against adopting the three signature features of his Order.

Relinquishment Is the Way to Holiness

It is my belief that people, consciously or not, desire something to live for—and not to "live for" only—but to sacrifice for, perhaps to die for. The sense is woven into the human fabric that there is a *reason* we are here, that our lives are not random. We belong to something, and the great challenge of human imagining is to winnow through the static noise of culture and take hold of the nub of truth as to why we exist. The key for Francis and those who followed him lay not in what one could attain as human pilgrims, but in what is freely relinquished for a higher aspiration. If St. Francis has taught me anything, he has taught me the value of what we *give up*. "Value" is not the right word, but it is as close as we can come to understanding that true power arises in what is freely relinquished. It is a force that is invisible and in some way immeasurable. Francis would assure us that there is great fulfillment to be had, but it does not arise through self-referring aspirations. It arises through self-relinquishment, giving things up, what some might call "mortifications." Because the more we shed of "self" the more we are postured to don the new attire of God's glory, an attire that is both invisible and intimate. It comes to us only in the act of open-palmed yielding.

I want to be clear that when I say "relinquishment" I am not entertaining thoughts of the kind of emptying espoused in Buddhism where relinquishment leads to nirvana, a state of "nothingness." In the Franciscan Way, "relinquishing" is the act of willingly giving up ownership of the terms of one's life and allegiances so that other new, higher, deeper, and more robust terms can realized. It is not an exercise to enter the realm of nothingness; it is an act of will that embraces a more pure form of holiness under the creative and robust operations of an intimate God, who requires something of us. Holiness is a mystery. It is attained only when the human will is surrendered to the operations of the Spirit of God. The limited human purview is not sufficient to wage a campaign toward holiness.

Thus, in the Franciscan Way, we are summoned to bow before him in humility and to accept whatever terms he asks of us in order to meet the challenge of his call upon us. I sit in my room and measure the parameters of my limited life and ponder my own insignificance and consider that we are all, in some way or another, fleeing the feeling of insignificance or feeling lost, depressed, or otherwise purposeless. What is the point? What is the purpose of our existence? Why are we here? What does it all mean? The beginning point of the answer to these age-old questions lies in our willingness to stop cleaving to our own version of what life means. Jesus said that whoever would save his life must lose it. In other words, let go of your ideas about what will save you. We cannot save ourselves, and the more we try, the farther we will wander from finding true salvation.

Franciscan Themes

There exist certain themes in Franciscan spirituality that enable any seeker to begin the process of wearing the mantle even if his or her station in life disallows adopting these strict vows. "The Franciscan Way" is a layperson's scheme for appropriating a unique quality of life, bearing its identity as Franciscan, yet opening a way for lay Catholics, lay Protestants, and even non-Christians to join that path. The Franciscan Way is not a religious Order; it is a way of life defined by key themes in Francis's understanding of God, creation, and humanity. All of this can be adopted by anyone desiring a deep and purifying spiritual ascent.

This book is laid out in three parts. Part One highlights the way Francis hijacked my own spiritual journey and shaped my later life. It also includes a brief biography of Francis. (Elsewhere and throughout the book, when dealing with biographical material, I refer frequently to portions drawn from my biography of St. Francis, titled *A Mended and Broken Heart, the Life and Love of Francis of Assisi.*[6]) Part Two examines the Franciscan vows—poverty, chastity, and obedience, exploring how these expressions can be understood and applied in modern times for those outside the official Order and in keeping with the spirit of the Third Order Franciscans. Part Three focuses on the virtues that Francis himself exalted and modeled for those who bore the name "Franciscan."

It is also important to note that, beyond the sentiments of St. Francis and St. Clare, I make generous use of insights from a variety of saints and spiritual writers. This is because the Franciscan Way, while built upon the apparatus of Franciscan operations and assertions, further embodies a willingness to glean insights from a wide fellowship of saints and strugglers, all of whom point the way to higher ground (spiritually speaking), as Francis himself did, and which his principles accommodate. Francis drew inspiration from many others who went before him, especially the Irish saints. So while the Franciscan principles put forth in this volume are built upon the bones that

Francis outlined for his Order, the lifeblood of its operations is embellished by a company of others who trod the pathway to holiness, among them St. Francis de Sales, Thomas Merton, and even Fred "Mister" Rogers.

If Franciscan spirituality is nothing else, it is an exercise in the particulars. Adopting these vows and cultivating the virtues enabled Francis and his followers to give concrete expression to these particulars and to grow in interior devotion in a uniquely Franciscan Way. I understand that living the Franciscan Way may not be for everyone. But it is the right fit for some, maybe you. Those on whom life has worked its ravages may find its consolations especially appealing. For those who desire spiritual ascent and greater clarity, the Franciscan Way shows a way forward—and not forward only but forward by means of miraculous, inexplicable, and invisible operations that ultimately land a striving soul in a place of peace, rest, and, in time, glory. If you find yourself in the unfortunate situation of having been betrayed, bereft, or otherwise overthrown by the "changes and chances of mortal life,"[7] the Franciscan Way bids you to hold on. Francis will find you even as he found me. You'll find your way through by the hand of a faithful, tested, and loving guide. It is my prayer that this short book will help you receive such graces.

Part One

FINDING FRANCIS

Now, at last, tired of being misled, entrust to the Truth
all that the Truth has given to you and nothing will be lost.
All that is withered in you will be made to thrive again.
All your sickness will be healed.
—St. Augustine

The moment that signaled my unwitting transition from conventional evangelical piety to "the Franciscan Way" occurred in a remote chapel nestled in the crag of a mountain above the town of Assisi. Francis himself had often retreated to this hermitage, also known as *Eremo delle Carceri* (Hermitage of the Caves). It was the year following my divorce, and I described it in a book I wrote at that time:

> . . . [W]e hiked the upper ridge of Mount
> Subasio, where Francis had walked many times.
> Hidden within its beech forests and down
> winding rocky pathways we took our lunch
> at a hermitage where Francis often retreated
> for solitude. I went into a chapel to pray, the
> only one there not bedecked in a nun's habit
> of black and white. Bending my aching legs
> to the hardwood kneeler, I knew I'd never be
> a nun. I was a hiker, in pain at the moment,
> my backpack near me on the pew, my boots
> scraping, shirt smelling, my walking stick
> within reach. I caught the breeze from an
> opened window and heard myself pray . . .
> "What does someone like me have to do with
> Francis?"

> The nuns didn't begrudge me my weeping. In a way, I wanted to laugh. I couldn't help thinking I'd taken on a life of poverty, chastity, and obedience without ever joining the Poor Clares![8]

The earliest days of my Christian sojourn were not marked by Franciscan devotion or even by Catholicism, but by evangelical pietism. I was a product of the "Jesus movement" of the 1970s, and the majority of my youth and early adult life was shaped by that faith expression. My spontaneous conversion in 1972 was both authentic and unsolicited. I had just turned 16 and sat alone on my bed in a state of great sorrow due to a variety of specific reasons. They were the same kinds of reasons for anyone's sorrow: damaged lives and practical consequences—children left crying alone on their beds.

The hand of God reached down from his heavenly seat and counted my tears as precious. He lifted my face, and the tears that fell thereafter bore the graces of the name of Jesus. I barely knew the name. I had no Bible. The *World Book Encyclopedia* sufficed to set me on my way. In time, the accoutrements of Christian devotion subsumed my life, and I embraced them wildly.

I became known among my peers as a Jesus Freak, a name I bore proudly. At that time, in the early 1970s, a new movement was arising, and I was a small part of it. The movement itself caused me to feel that I was part of something big—at least bigger than my insignificant life. It was written of in major media: "The Year of the Evangelical," and so forth. Anyway, the seed of faith had been planted that day on my bed, and thereafter forces began to do their work with the effect of bringing forth a form of life that defined my days.

In order for a seed to germinate, that is, for the external shell to yield to the force of life arising out of it, certain conditions must be met. In the case of the seed of my newly emerging faith, those conditions moved from what I gleaned from the *World*

Book Encyclopedia to acquiring a real Bible, I don't remember how or from whom. Nor do I remember which version I read. At that time the notion of Bible "versions" was beyond me. I attended a national youth conference at which I heard Billy Graham speak and where my faith became strangely animated by the idea of reading a small booklet outlining simple "laws" to total strangers, people in movie theaters, that would translate their hopeless lives to a world of light and abundance, right there in the fifth row holding a box of popcorn. I also found a dynamic young church where the pastor's preaching felt like cleansing water on a parched soul. These conditions surrounded that living seed, and a life burst forth in the form of evangelical devotion. Enthusiasms heightened, being tempered only slightly by words spoken by Billy Graham at the youth conference that struck me then and strike me still: "It is not easy to be a New Testament Christian." Of course then I took it to mean that the person in the movie theater to whom I was presenting the spiritual laws would turn a cold shoulder and rebuff me. It did mean that, alas. But it meant much more than that too, as comes to be understood by any Christian who perseveres.

My evangelical fervor underwent a great reckoning when my 24-year marriage to a pastor collapsed. Here I must digress in order to lay bare the contours of a broken life that set the stage for the spiritual turn I was to take under the tutelage of St. Francis.

Things Fall Apart

Tolstoy said all happy families are alike, and each unhappy family is unhappy in its own way. The same is true of marriages and, alas, the dissolution of marriages. Each dissolution is unhappy in its own way, and the dissolution of an evangelical-Christian marriage is perhaps the unhappiest of all. It is a sorrow that finds little solace in the world. Two people, who in a declaration under God have abided as one and forged an original and unique existence, suffer ruination before the eyes of horrified onlookers, be they friends or family. Pat Conroy in his essay "Anatomy of a

Divorce"[9] says divorces should be conducted in "abattoirs, surgical wards, blood banks or funeral homes." Yet they are played out in real time amid colonies of real people, human souls whose inner moorings will be forever altered. There is no uncreating what was made in a marriage and which, in divorce, is unmade.

When my husband and I married as young college students, we held out all the optimism of youth and zeal for evangelical devotion. We set our course toward mission and service and bent all decisions to that end.

As we pursued such noble aspirations—he in ministry and I in writing—gritty details of our actual life were unfolding in hidden moments and darkened corners. These were batted away in deference to our higher callings. The Christian marriage calls for long-suffering, and Christians are to be credited for holding so high a view of the holy estate. This standard, coupled with the immediate arrival of three children sequentially in our life, meant that cultivating proper bounds and healthier attitudes in our already-troubled marriage was overthrown by sheer management of daily life. By the time we graduated from seminary, we were parents of three boys under the age of four.

Over the span of the next twenty-plus years, the negative patterns that started as mere kernels, being left unaddressed, grew disproportionately, and, over time, became the apparatus of our marriage. On this point I am reminded of the words of St. Francis de Sales, who said, "Small mistakes made at the beginning of any project grow infinitely great as it progresses."[10] The only way to end these patterns was to dismantle the apparatus. For many years that price felt too high.

As our marital breakdown was reaching its nadir, death became an abiding theme in my mind, and I pondered it. Thoughts overtook me pertaining to my own death. In the darkest corners of my troubled mind at that time, I felt as if my death would have solved everything. This is because the death of a pastor's wife in the midst of marital collapse is preferable (so I thought) to the ignominy of a Christian divorce. Death would have been the way out of the contradictions. When you feel there is no way out, you want to end it.

There is death enough that takes place in the dissolution of a long-standing Christian marriage. For a time it seems all death, a sea of death. Death of the vows. Death of the ballast of "home," where your grown children and grandchildren can gather. Death of your obituary reading "loving wife." Death of being a role model. There were so many deaths, I entertained the distorted thinking that my physical death would have been preferable.

The evangelical system in which I found myself—both in the context of a failing marriage and in the aftermath of its demise—touted all things "biblical"—things such as the sun ought not to go down on one's anger,[11] and we ought to admonish one another in songs, hymns, and spiritual songs,[12] and a husband ought to love his wife as he loves his own body.[13] The system upheld these notions in theory, and I expected the system to stay true in real life. I relied upon the system to do so. Over the span of my youth and in my early adulthood, I had raised a spear to fight for such devotion, glory with glory and flame with flame. I continued to think this was the way it ought to be and was destined to be, because I believed the principles and functioned devotedly within the stated rules.

Yet it is unpleasant in the extreme for a man of the cloth to be embroiled in a situation that demands naked honesty in order for truth and healing to be surmounted. Such naked honesty is too much to ask of the lead man in the cog of a finely tuned and organized social and theological system.

In fact, the system itself over the decades of our marriage precluded an honest reckoning. The system lent oxygen to the beast, keeping it in hiding, and imposed on me the obligation to keep things going, to keep honoring.

Four years before our marriage ended, I called the chair of the elder board of my husband's church late one night. I asked for his and the church's help. Our marriage was not what it appeared on Sundays, I said. We were facing serious, incapacitating struggles in the marriage that cannot be overcome without third-party intervention, and this is what I was asking from the leaders of my husband's church. This elder, however, did not deem my solicitation for help as warranting redress; I never heard from him again, nor did he again look me in the eye. (I learned later that this dismissal was prompted by my husband waving off further inquiry.) The system made me "wear my blacks" until a kind of withering overtook my onetime impassioned soul. Writer Annie Dillard, in one of her books, quoted a marine biologist who described the anomalous behavior of a type of starfish that, under circumstances of duress, would begin to pull itself apart. Dillard said that it would seem that in an animal that deliberately pulls itself apart we have "the very acme of something or other." Like the starfish in Dillard's book, I dismembered myself. I tore out my own heart in order to end the contradictions.

I had reached the nadir point. I had once felt strongly about matters of faith and piety. I had raised my spear to fight for them. Now such enthusiasms were extinguished. There was nothing left there. I laid down my spear. My belief in that system turned to sorrow and regret. The system proved counterproductive. The system ruined my life.

It was at this point that I traveled to Umbria, Italy, with my sister as a means to begin the rehabilitation of my life in the aftermath of my divorce. Umbria is a landlocked agricultural region in central Italy where rolling mountains surround an alluvial plain dotted with cypress and elms, mulberries, olive groves, and vineyards. On the third day of that trip our small hiking group ascended a rugged grassy hillside to an isolated medieval fortress known as *Le Due Torri*, the two towers. On this summit an eleventh-century farm house and a small chapel rested in the shadows of two watchtowers. In the Middle Ages these towers would have defended the region against marauders. It was also a stopping place along "the pilgrim's road" that cut through Umbria, north to south, a route traveled on foot by pilgrims from all over Europe, including, tradition says, the apostles Peter and Paul. The notion of "pilgrimage" was especially robust during the Middle Ages, as lowly sojourners in brown capes, leather sandals, and black hats set out on foot in pursuit of the "holy destinations": Rome, Jerusalem, and Santiago de Compostela in Spain. It was not an easy time to be alive in central Italy, given the violence and instability of the age. Times were more daunting for pilgrims, who would plod rugged paths over jutting ridges in bracing winds, seasonal rains, and sometimes even snow with warring factions at their heels. *Le Due Torri* was directly in the path of the primary pilgrimage road through Umbria in the eleventh, twelfth, and thirteenth centuries, and it was a resting spot for pilgrims.

As we prepared to depart, our host took me to the small chapel set off from the towers. Made of whitewashed limestone, it stood little more than twelve feet square with a half dozen pews and a small central altar. "Would Saint Francis have visited here?" I asked. "Of course—everyone knows he was a pilgrim," he answered earnestly. "He walked everywhere. It is probable he stopped here. This location is on the way to many places. We have no records. But we believe he was probably here." This moment awakened a curiosity inside me, and I became convinced this journey was linked to the person of Francis of Assisi. It signaled the beginning of what would become my late-in-life journey along the Franciscan Way.

On the last morning in Assisi during that trip I made my way alone in the early light down to the little church of San Damiano, the one Francis had rebuilt in accordance with a vision he received while praying there (to be noted in the next chapter). Here he had established the Poor Clares (his "Little Brothers" being located nearby at another church he'd rebuilt). It was to San Damiano, and to Clare, that Francis retreated near the end of his life, when illness and blindness had nearly incapacitated him.

San Damiano is a mile south of Assisi's walls, tucked beyond an olive grove. That morning, a mist fell over the valley, and the clouds hung low over Mount Subasio. Nearing the little church, I passed a stone with words carved into its face: *Il Signore ti dia pace,* "the Lord give you peace," Francis's well-known greeting.

I found a spot under a tree behind the church near a cistern. With birds about me and morning's light glinting off the dew of olive trees, I thought of Clare, whom Francis had brought here. Some say they had loved each other but had renounced it. I thought of a question I'd like to put to Francis in my imagination: *How does one finish a life with wounds?*

I heard nuns singing from inside the walls, the same walls Francis built when the voice said, "Rebuild my church." He had been given a task. He accepted a humble responsibility. From that church where I now sat, the image of the Crucified One brought him purpose and rescued him. So he picked up a stone. Then he picked up another stone. When he could find none, he begged for stones. At long last, as I noted in my memoir, "Stone upon stone, amid olive groves and singing birds, cooled by morning mists, he moved and piled and scraped until the stones became a wall. The wall became a church. The church became an assertion."[14]

This trip and these moments awakened me to a new possibility for what it might mean to walk in faith. In these early moments of this new journey, Francis was showing me that true power can arise from who we are not, and dependency covers what we can't do, and surprises await letting go of what we can't keep. I didn't see it as surrender, but consecration—even expansion—of my soul, like praying open-armed, dying a death with your face in the dirt and making it a benediction. G. K. Chesterton said that in writing his biography of Francis, he (Chesterton) was "certain of failure." Even so, he was "not altogether overcome by fear," because, he said, Francis "suffered fools gladly." Being the fool is the only way to find Francis. That is because he went where fools go. He called himself God's greatest fool.

I ponder the metaphor of the flower, which captures the essence of the awkward, sometimes painful, but ultimately transformative metamorphosis. The outward form of a flower withers and dies. It then invisibly transfers its life energy to the dormant seed that in turn rises in a new form of life. In the same way, even as the outward form of my brand of Christian devotion shriveled, the essence of my early faith lay dormant as in a buried seed. By the graces of the Spirit, the death of one "flower" became the life of the seed that blossomed into a new flower. This is how the Franciscan Way took root, nourished the dormant seed, and bloomed in my later life.

As I noted in the Introduction, I share this part of my life's journey not to elevate my story but to lay bare the level of human desolation I confronted in a way that might offer hope for others whose lives, for whatever reasons, have similarly collapsed. The point is that collapse isn't the end of your story. It is the beginning of a new story. The way back to becoming a fully formed, functioning, and (I dare say) beautiful new creation comes through sometimes painful exertions. It is an exercise of will that overthrows all previous ingrained reactions and habits. All things are being made new.[15] As Francis de Sales put it, "Keep walking—we say to these souls so desirous of their perfection—walking the way of your vocation with simplicity, more intent on doing than on desiring; that is the shortest road."[16]

WHO WAS FRANCIS?

A man has as much knowledge as he executes.
—Francis of Assisi

In order to fully grasp the transformative power of the Franciscan Way, it is necessary to understand the rock from which it was hewn. Who was Francis? What motivated him, and what forces conspired to transform him?

Francesco Bernadone had been a happy youth, born in 1182 in the medieval fortressed city-state of Assisi, Italy, a mountain town that spilled down the southern slope of Mount Subasio. He was the son of a wealthy cloth merchant, Pietro Bernardone, and his French wife, Pica. His father had been away on business at the time of his birth, so his mother, being a religious woman, named him Giovanni, after John the Baptist. Upon his father's return, however, he renamed the child Francesco—"the French one"—a name that carried a father's dreams to carry on the family business selling linens in France. (Unlike his wife, Pietro was not a religious man.) Falling under the influence of his mother and being further exposed to French styles and tradition through the merchant trade of his father, Francis styled himself after the troubadours, singing their songs and embracing their idealized romanticism. The troubadours were poets who traveled the countryside making melodies of love's tender longings, and Francis sang their songs and embraced their idealism.

Despite being of a diminutive build (he was approximately 5'3" tall), his large, kind eyes and happy disposition made him a popular favorite among the town's youth. He apprenticed to his father in the cloth business and happily assumed the role of trendsetter for

French silks and velvets of extravagant colors. The friends of his youth, when they'd been drinking—which was often—called him our "*dominus*," our king. Francis would sing for them in French and buy another round of drinks. More than once the name of the young son of Bernadone passed through the lips of gossips and barkeeps. He was the leader of a "wild pack of Assisi youths," as one historian puts it, adding, "This was a sexually anarchic era, and the town was full of randy, undisciplined and hedonistic youngsters. [I]t would be difficult to think of him as diverging from his comrades in only this one area of adolescent experimentation."[17] Even so, Francis was well-liked. His extravagant generosity and courtesy extended to all, including the poor.

During the unsettling period when Francis was growing up in Italy, feudalism was in full bloom, and violence was ingrained in medieval culture. Assisi was not exempt. In fact, Assisi was well known for its feisty and riotous rush to arms. As in other fortress towns, locals in Assisi celebrated weapons and carnage in festivities. A springtime festival called *Calendimaggio* involved men from the upper part of town (the nobles) and those from the lower part (the merchants), who would meet in the main piazza with blunted arms. No-holds-barred mayhem would inevitably break out between the warring neighbors, ratcheting up the stakes of the game to outright battle. Young lads followed the lead of their older heroes, joining the contest and learning the art of combat. The games persisted until one side conceded defeat after a dozen or more participants had been maimed or killed. Since this was entertainment, the loss of life and limb was mere bad luck, and families could not exact revenge.

Ambition for war was endemic in the culture, while the power to orchestrate it lay only with the overlords in the castles, the nobility. For a long time, this consigned the players in the social arena to one of two roles: landing-owning feudal nobility with its attendant warrior class (knights) and the subject peoples—serfs—who served through subjugation and intimidation. The privilege of making war belonged to the nobility exclusively. For the merchant class, knighthood could be attained, but only through combat. So, the rising merchant class grew restless. As Francis grew, a theme arose in his heart to win knighthood in keeping with the idealism of the troubadours.

Assisi was strategically located along the primary route between Rome and France, the *Strada Francesca*. Tradesmen from Italy traveled this road endlessly, south to north, and Pietro Bernadone, Francis's father, stood out as among the region's most prosperous merchants. He was a clothier, buying and selling linens in Champagne and Provence. Pietro and other sellers would return to their hometowns with colorful stories of wars and uprisings in France, such as the revolt of the merchant class that occurred in Picardy and Flanders. The people there were taking up arms and throwing the nobles out, marking the beginning of a trend that would sweep across the medieval landscape—the rise of the *commune*, which portended the demise of feudalism. The Italian merchants, or *mediani*, spurred the movement, aspiring to win their share of the prize—upward mobility—heretofore claimed exclusively by the nobility. Their means of asserting their claim was to make war. In fact, because making war carried the association of winning knighthood, for the *mediani*, this made war poetic. And Francis, being a poet, rallied around the aspiration. The second half of the twelfth century—as Francis was coming of age—saw the repulsion of the imperial feudal entrenchment strike most ferociously. Local towns waged self-contained class wars.

The impulse for battle carried across city limits into neighboring localities. Local wars between rival cities defined the age as much as intracity class revolt. Combat was woven into the fabric of everyday life. Killing one's enemy (at least one) became a rite of passage and a test of moral grit. Venice fought Genoa. Genoa fought Pisa. Pisa fought Lucca. Lodi fought Milan. Faenza fought Ravenna. Florence fought Siena. Assisi fought Perugia. These were the times in which Francis lived.

Assisi went to war two times during Francis's youth, and in his effort to earn knighthood, he fought ferociously in both conflicts. The first took place in 1198 when Francis would have been 16, during a time of great tumult in Assisi as the *mediani* rose up against the nobility—known as the *maggiore*. The former were ready to claim independence from the heavy hand of the latter in the name of the *commune*. At an opportune moment, when the town's civic leader (kind of like the mayor) was absent, Assisi's merchant-class warriors, 16-year-old Francis among them, laid siege to the town's fortress, La Rocca. Pulling stone after stone from the white rugged walls, they dismantled and razed the fortress. Thus began a civil war in Assisi that soon spilled onto the city streets, where the *mediani* routed castles and other strongholds of feudalism, driving noble families from their homes. Many nobles fled Assisi for its hated rival city, Perugia, due west. Clare's family and Clare herself were among those driven from their homes.

The second war occurred four years later, in approximately 1202, when Francis was 20. This melee arose against the neighboring city-state of Perugia, when the displaced *Assisiani* nobles decided to return and reclaim their homes. Bold and brash as the young *Assisiani* warriors were, including Francis, they were badly outflanked and more or less slaughtered on the field between the two cities. Many of Francis's friends numbered among the dead, and he himself was taken prisoner in Perugia. He languished for a year underground with little food, bad water, cold conditions, and no latrine. There he contracted malaria that would plague him the rest of his days, and probably also the bone tuberculosis pathologists recently determined afflicted him. After a year's imprisonment, his father negotiated a ransom for his release. Francis remained bedridden in recovery for another year. He was never the same.

For a brief stint after his recovery he tried in vain to recapture the bliss of his profligate youth, but his heart was not in it. He wrestled with depression. In a grand but futile attempt to attain his desired aspiration of knighthood, in 1205 he joined the papal forces of Walter of Brienne on a Crusade. Barely twenty miles south of Assisi, however, his malarial fever disabled him. He returned home in despair, weakened by illness and shamed by the sorrow of failed dreams.

During this season of malaise, at the age of 23, while on an errand for his father, he passed a run-down church called San Damiano a mile south of Assisi and stopped to rest inside its crumbling walls. Sitting beneath a Syrian cross hanging over the altar bearing the image of the crucified Christ, Francis perceived the image was speaking to him. "Francis," it said, "don't you see that my house is being destroyed? Go, then, and rebuild it."

This encounter initiated not only a building campaign that Francis undertook singlehandedly, but more, it began a great reversal wherein his life's goals and priorities would be forever upended.

It is during this period, I believe, that Francis began his friendship with Clare, which bloomed into romantic love.[18] The next two or three years of his life are shrouded in mystery, though a few points find general agreement. The first is, Francis's experience with war, prison, and illness tempered him. The second is, this tempering, over the subsequent few years, led to his renunciation of family, his conversion to the gospel, and ultimately his embracing a life of poverty. I hasten to add that the term "conversion" is not universally accepted by all Franciscans. Some prefer the term "penitence," the term Francis himself used when describing his change. In either case, the end result was the same. Finally, third, it is also agreed upon and documented in the early sources that there was indeed a valid secondary agent who, as Francis began to move in a new direction toward God, helped him along the way. The friend, whose name is not known, stood by him throughout the two years of tortured inner battles, flesh against spirit, which were described by his contemporary and poet, Henri d'Avranches:

> He has a kind of debate with himself: Do more
> things exist in the mind
> than what he perceives with his senses? There's an
> unequal strife
> in his soul, as sense-perception from beneath assaults
> the peak of his reasoning.
> Sense holds out feasts, allurements of love,
> wealth and high honor and human approval—but
> cannot go any further.
> Reason holds out life without end, delights in that
> City Above,
> paradise joy, mysterious song, unspeakable light. . . .
> One moment his mind is up in the air
> and again it is down on the ground. . . .[19]

Francis's first biographer, Thomas of Celano, says Francis took this special unidentified friend "to remote places, places well-suited for counsel, telling him that he had found a certain precious and great treasure." This friend rejoiced and "willingly accompanied Francis whenever he was asked." They would go frequently and secretly to a special cave, or grotto, toward Mount Subasio where they would talk about "this treasure." I make the case in my biography that this secret friend was Clare and that she was intimately instrumental in his drawn-out and at times tortured conversion.[20]

Whether or not this special friend was indeed Clare, it is impossible to understand the life of Francis without confronting this relationship. For me, as a researcher, it meant examining censored material, wading through hagiographies, noting the gaps, questioning the gaps, assimilating contradictory responses, taking note of questions that evoke uncomfortable pauses, darting eyes, or outright laughter. It means asking logical questions. The official Catholic position asserts that the bond between Francis and Clare, while extraordinary, is likened to that of a father and daughter. For this they cite the alleged age difference: It is widely agreed that Francis was born in 1182 (some say 1181); Clare's birth date is unknown. It is thought to be in or around 1192 or 1193 or 1194.[21] Some also cite the fact that Clare was of the nobility while Francis was part of the rising merchant class, which would have been an impediment and precluded their having known one another during their early years. I demur noting that Assisi was a very small town; Clare was the town beauty and Francis (for a time) was the town playboy. It defies common logic to suggest that these two stand-outs did not at some point come into one another's sphere.

The problem for researchers trying to understand Clare lies in the fact that the little historical knowledge we have of Clare herself is derived largely from the early Franciscan documents, most of which interpreted her life through the life of St. Francis. Even in these early writings, however, mention of Clare began to disappear over time. Franciscan scholar Paschal Robinson noted despairingly: "Not a few [records] were destroyed; others disappeared. As far as dates go, only one—the date of her canonization—is given. Save for a few fragments of pious legend not one of the early sources gives us the year of Saint Clare's birth. . . . [W]e are without any exact knowledge of the life of Saint Clare down to 1212."[22]

Yet, while little can be validated historically about Clare herself except for the year of her canonization (1255), we know plenty about her family. Her paternal great-great-grandfather was a nobleman named Offredo. Her great-grandfather was Bernardino. Her grandfather thus was called Offreduccio di Bernardo, a powerful count. Offreduccio had three sons, Scipione di Offreduccio, Monaldo, and Favorone, Clare's father. "They were all strong, daring, cruel, known for their bravura in the use of the spear and the halberd." Clare's father was a knight known to ride into battle with a drawn sword. The family descended from the Lombards and Franks and was connected to and supportive of the emperor Frederick of Barbarossa[23] and distantly related to the popes of the period.

Clare's mother, Ortolana, also of noble lineage, was linked to the same German line from which arose Frederick II, Barbarossa's grandson. Clare had two sisters, Catherine (later called Agnes) and Beatrice. The family lived in the piazza of San Rufino, the northern part of town where the nobles lived, the part of town that came under siege during Assisi's civil war. As noted, Clare's family was forced to flee. Her father was very involved in this uprising, so he wasn't home much. We know Clare was beautiful and that by her early teens was being prepared and courted for marriage, and that all offers were rebuffed. She was quiet, demur, and big-hearted toward the poor.

During one of my chats with a friar when I was living in Assisi, he posed the question, "What was the internal energy that changed Francis?" It's a logical question, and I had spent a great deal of time wondering the same thing. I contemplated inexplicable gaps where there ought to have been a record. I met with contradictions, bizarre rationalizations, and special pleading. So I asked: What is at stake if the "secret friend" was Clare? What if, in keeping with the culture of courtly love that so enamored Francis, she had inspired his final failed attempt to attain the glory for knighthood, consoling him and urging him to seek God? What if, after seeking God, Francis found him and thus began an internal turnaround that would torment him for a few more few years? What if Clare had been the "internal energy" that changed him?

The turning point for Francis, which marked the end of his tortured equivocation and a full and wild embrace of the life of a penitent, occurred on the road while he was on an errand for his father. Up to this point he had been hounded by a summons to follow a new way of living in the footsteps of Jesus, but was struggling. He was still bound to his worldly appetites both in station and lifestyle. He had been a party boy driven by carnal impulses and worldly aspirations. Yet, that day, on the road south of Assisi, the moment arrived when the Spirit of God bore down and drove him to make a choice. That moment came in the form of the leper's rattle.

In order to grasp the significance of this moment for Francis, it is critical to understand the place of lepers in medieval times. Lepers, rich or poor, were outcasts, generally reviled and isolated from society. They were consigned to live out their days in leper hospitals, which were foul and fetid places to which no normal human being would willingly submit. Neither did many of the infected persons. In that case they would often be snitched upon by fearful neighbors, friends, and sometimes family members. The leper would be removed from his or her home, forever banished from day-to-day life. Upon arrival at such places the incoming resident would go before the priest to make his vow. The priest would proclaim:

> Dear poor little man of a good God, by means of great sadness and tribulation of sickness, of leprosy, and of many other miseries, one gains the kingdom of heaven where there is no sickness or sorrow and all is pure and white, without stain, more brilliant than the sun. You will go there, if it pleases God. In the meantime, be a good Christian, bear with patience this adversity and God will be merciful to you.[24]

Anyone who came into contact with a leper would thus himself be deemed unclean. That is why lepers were sequestered from the comings and goings of average citizens. It is also why lepers were forced to carry a rattle, or *tentennella,* as it was called, so as to warn others of their presence and alert them to go another way.

On this occasion, Francis had gone south of town to settle accounts on land owned by his father. Upon his return, he heard the sound of the leper's rattle. This stopped him in his tracks. On any other such occasion Francis would have turned on his heels and run in the opposite direction. He noted later, near the end of his life, recounting his conversion in his *Testament*:

> When I was in sin, the sight of lepers nauseated me beyond measure. But then God himself led me into their company, and I had pity on them.

As the leper continued on his way, the would-be knight dismounted from his horse and "with the strength of youth and the speed of a horse, ran to the leper and pulled his rotting flesh to his arms."[25]

> When I had once become acquainted with them, what had previously nauseated me became a source of spiritual and physical consolation for me. After that I did not wait long before leaving the world.[26]

Francis's embrace of the leper turned his world upside-down. In this singular gesture, Francis made a decisive break from the patterns and habits of his life, putting himself in a place of willing vulnerability and utter dependence upon God, as now his identity lay with the outcasts. Embracing the leper put to death his fleshly impulses because now, he too was numbered among the "unclean." As his biographer Henri d'Avranches described it, after that, *Franciscum scilicet omnen.* "Francis changed utterly": "Envy is wiped out by kindliness, and patience eliminates anger; gluttony falls by sobriety, libido by purity."[27]

Beyond the physical breakage of his carnal impulses, the place of the leper in Francis's understanding of the Kingdom of God proved a defining feature of the Franciscan Way. As I note in my biography of Francis, his vision of the gospel turned the prevailing social order governed by the Church on its head. At the time, the pope, bishops, and church officials stood at the center of the organizing apparatus of societal order, and all deference and honor went to them. Yet, Francis's identity—and eventually that of his Order—placed those on the social fringe front and center in the priorities of God and of his mission. The popularity of his movement could thus have been seen as tantamount to a call to revolution against the Church. Indeed, some of his later followers interpreted his teachings this way. Yet in truth the only revolt Francis had in mind was the invitation to bring the outcast in from the edges and place him front and center in the family of God.

Thus, with the leper's embrace, the revolution that would define the Franciscan movement was launched. Francis would never be the same, nor—it could be said—would the landscape of his times and the operations of the Church.

Now that Francis was fully committed to his life as a penitent, we return to the ruins of San Damiano, when he was given the command to "rebuild my church." This meant for Francis that in the early days of his religious life he undertook building projects, for which, we know from the sources, Clare was supporting him financially.[28] He worked first at repairing San Damiano, which he intended from the start to house women.[29] When this was complete he moved on to two other properties, the Porziuncula, a half-mile away, which became the seat of his Order (and where he lived for a time), and then also a small church called San Pietro della Spina, which has been lost. At this point in his life he had assumed the penitent's tunic and sandals and begged for bread and also for stones with which to build. But he had not yet given shape to his convictions in the way of forming a religious Order. He simply chose for himself to live as a penitent.

The building activity began to attract the attention of the locals in Assisi, who had known Francis as a clothier, an aspiring knight, and a ladies' man—but not as a beggar. Some townspeople, predictably, dismissed him as mad. Others were moved by his humility, tenacity, and happiness in the face of poverty and ridicule. He began to be approached by citizens of rank who had become curious about his work. (This is discussed at length in the upcoming chapter on poverty.)

In due course, as often happens with charismatic champions who launch unusual movements, Francis developed a fellowship that centered around certain ways of living but which ultimately led to a uniquely identified "Franciscan" cohort of followers. This unusual band not only stood out from other penitential movements that marked the age, but they also forged a new path for those who desired to live a different kind of life that reflected devotion and obedience to the radical nature of Francis's example. I say "radical," because in the Franciscan sense, the kind of life he and his followers embodied went to the root of human striving. This, in equal measure, repulsed some and attracted others. This curiosity would eventually explode into a following that required that he secure papal approval and adopt a Rule for governance. This meant, for him, years of struggle and turmoil in the effort to bring an unwieldy movement into some kind of order. (This is also discussed in upcoming chapters.)

The later years of his short life were marked by turmoil, illness, and feelings of failure. He had traveled to Egypt to convert the sultan al-Malik al-Kamil, but failed (though he won his friendship).[30] In his final two years, his eyesight was fading; he couldn't bear to be in daylight. His brotherhood was in crisis, as some thought Francis's claim on the gospel was too unreasonable. At one point he feared his own Order would expel him. "Maybe I should rejoice if they throw me out in shame," he said. "Perhaps it would profit my soul."

Near the end of his life, he retreated to San Damiano under the watchcare of Clare. Despite his blindness robbing him of seeing the sun's light and the beauty of field grass and flowers, he composed a song in praise of the beauty and glory of God's creation:

Altissimo—Most High—
No man is worthy to speak Your name.

All praise be Yours, my Lord, through all Your creatures,
And first my lord Brother Sun,
who brings the day and You give us light through him.
He is beautiful and radiant with his great splendor,
giving witness of You, most High.

At the end of Francis's life, age 44, his liver and spleen were distended with lesions, and malarial parasites made him vomit. He found it hard to breathe. The paradox was that even in suffering, his death became an assertion of consecration. As his final gesture on this earth, he requested of his brothers, "When you see that I have come to the end, put me out naked on the ground and allow me to lie there for as long as it takes to walk a leisurely mile."

They laid him naked, face down, and he wept with gratitude, embracing God's beauty with his face in the dirt. He whispered to a brother, "I have done what is mine to do. May Christ teach you what is yours to do."

Part Two

VOWS

INTRODUCTION TO THE VOWS

Let all of us guard against all pride and vainglory,
and keep ourselves from the wisdom of this world.
For the prompting of the flesh
seeks and strives to be full of talk,
but cares little for action;
and seeks not God-centeredness and holiness in the inner man,
but looks for and desires a religiosity and
holiness that can be seen by men. . . .
The Spirit of the Lord
strives instead for humility and patience
and for the pure and simple and true peace of the inner man.[31]
—St. Francis of Assisi

An Exercise in the Particulars

Franciscan spirituality is nothing if it is not an exercise in the particulars. Francis's theology didn't mean believing in something generally; it meant believing specifically and then manifesting that belief concretely.

This is evident foremost in the three signature vows he demanded of his followers. It could be said that the vows for Francis were the self-imposed external mechanism, from the top down, functioning as a wedge to be jammed into the gears of human self-destruction to halt the descent into despair. They echo the thought expressed by Peter in his first letter, "whoever suffers is finished with sin."[32]

The Vows

The three Franciscan vows of poverty, chastity, and obedience reflect the concrete nature of Franciscan devotion. Each in its own way required decisive action in an immediate sense that showed itself in the outworking of the way one lived his or her life. The vows were the firewall against half-hearted devotion. Anyone who desired to follow Francis was expected to apply these exertions as a show of fealty and humility.

In time, as his movement grew, and as Francis reckoned with the reality that its growth required him to bring it into order, he crafted a short document to present to the pope in order to gain his favor and validation of his small band of mendicants. This first document was comprised mainly of biblical texts from the Gospels and was organized under Francis's personal authority. It has been lost, so it is not known if the vows were included. Nevertheless, in time, as the Order grew, the brothers needed a more extensive and cogent document that included broader parameters and clearer definitions, and one that was less dependent on Francis's personal authority. In the first draft, known as the Early Rule of 1221, the three vows were front and center, appearing in the first paragraph, defining parameters of his Order:

> The Rule and life of the friars is to live in obedience, in chastity and without property, following the teaching of our Lord Jesus Christ who says, "If you would be perfect, go sell what you have and give to the poor and you shall have treasure in heaven; and come and follow me" (Matthew 19:21).[33]

The Rule of 1221 was revised two years later in 1223, the latter becoming the standing Rule that still governs the Order today. Here too, the vows are noted in the opening sentence of the first paragraph: "The Rule and life of the Friars Minor is this, namely to observe the Holy Gospel of our Lord Jesus Christ by living in obedience, without property, and in chastity."[34]

The seriousness with which Francis upheld this code is evidenced in an episode that took place in the early days of the Order. When the brothers were living at a location known as Rivo Torto, a brother had joined them who, according to Francis's close companion Brother Leo, "prayed little and did no work, and never went begging (for he was ashamed), but he ate well." Leo continued:

> Considering his behavior, Blessed Francis was warned by the Holy Spirit that this brother was a sensual man. One day he said to him: 'Go your way, Brother Fly, for you wish to eat the fruit of the labor of your brothers, while you remain idle in the vineyard of God. You resemble Brother Drone who gathers nothing, does no work, but eats the fruit of the activity of the working bees.' He left without asking forgiveness, for he was a sensual man.[35]

When discussing the Franciscan vows in the context of a religious forum one time, I was asked in a confrontational way by a Protestant Evangelical, *How can you uphold Francis as an example when his view on human sexuality was so abhorrent to the standard Christian view of marriage and procreation?* His point was well taken. But at the same time, this questioner misconstrued the operations of (in this case) the vow of chastity and Francis's purpose for imposing it. As the biographical narrative of Francis's life reflects, he had a very real problem with the flesh and its carnal impulses (not unlike St. Augustine). He was a slave to them. Once he had experienced deliverance from this affliction on the occasion of his embracing the leper, he understood the power that misapplied sexual impulses can wield over a human soul, even a soul striving for holiness.

So, in keeping with the operations of the vows, he imposed upon those who would join his Order the dictate that a life in the flesh was incompatible with a life among the Friars Minor. His reasons were specific, concrete, and, it could be argued, legitimate. He was not expecting such constraints to be imposed upon all people who desired to live "the Franciscan Way." However, he did expect it of those who desired to join the First Order of the Friars Minor.

It is important to note at this point that Francis abhorred excessive physical mortifications such as those that marked some other penitential movements of the time. He forbade his brothers to engage in self-flagellation and other forms of self-harm. In this way, it would be wrong to think of him as an extreme ascetic. While he understood that there is a place for exercising restraint and self-denial on certain points, he never allowed these disciplines to show themselves in abject self-torture. His love of God's creation (as will be explicitly explored in the chapter on the virtue of wisdom), his vision of its beauty and glory, and his seeing every aspect of creation as a gift from God forbade him from allowing any hint of self-harm or self-torture, even if it is undertaken as a "spiritual discipline" to mortify the flesh.

This inevitably begs the question: How can a person live "the Franciscan Way" while not appropriating in the strictest sense the demands of the vows that Francis imposed? In the following chapters of this section it is my hope to answer that question.

CHAPTER ONE
POVERTY

Holy Poverty consecrates worldly goods.

In order to journey steadily, we must apply ourselves to
doing well the stretch of road immediately before us
and not waste time wanting to do the last lap. . . .
Look straight in front of you and not at
those dangers you see in the distance.
To you they look like armies, but they
are only willow branches
and while you are looking at them,
you may take a false step.[36]
—Francis de Sales

When considering "poverty" as among the highest attributes of Franciscan spirituality, the tendency is to envision the iteration by which Francis himself embodied it—stripping naked in the town square where, in dramatic fashion, he remitted to his bewildered father his stylish French frock, donning instead a rugged tunic with ashes on his head and henceforth refusing to touch money. Inevitably, such envisioning reduces serious thought of taking this vow to a strictly intellectual exercise, since so few rational adults would dream of emulating Francis's model in real life. One may find his gestures interesting, or perhaps compelling, but in the end, it is only natural that one would deem such a goal as ultimately unattainable.

There is no getting around the fact that when Francis laid out the terms of his movement and placed a vow of poverty as its signature feature, he did not simply mean "poverty of spirit," though that had its place, as will be seen. He meant that whatever money is held in the bank or in real estate or in whatever form, is to be gotten rid of—and not simply handed off to relatives. He meant that it is to be meted out to the infirm, the dispossessed, or the outcast. He carried out to the letter the words Jesus spoke to the young man of great wealth: "If you want to be complete, go, sell what you own, and give the money to the poor. Then you will have treasure in heaven. And come follow me."[37]

One of the most astonishing aspects of studying Francis's movement is not the strictness of this code; it is the sheer numbers of people, men and women and many of great wealth and rank, who embraced it wholeheartedly to the very letter of Francis's dictate.

A History of Franciscan Poverty

The first such example occurred early on in Francis's post-conversion life with the curiosity of a wealthy man of arms named Bernardo di Quintavalle.[38] He had been a respected member of the wealthy class and was a man of letters. He held degrees in civil and canon law and owned a home in Assisi not far from Francis's family home. He was approximately the same age as Francis and probably fought with him in battle, though he would not have been numbered among the rabble that crowned Francis "king of the party" in earlier days. Bernardo had led a measured and respectable civic life. It is evident he watched from a distance as surprising changes overtook the one-time party-loving son of Bernardone, and he couldn't make sense of them. He harbored questions. More than once, he invited Francis to stay in his home in Assisi seeking answers, and Francis gladly accepted. Bernardo understood that the townspeople were calling Francis crazy. Yet during these intimate conversations Bernardo saw that Francis's bearing was sound and he expressed himself lucidly.

The legends say that one night when Francis was staying in Bernardo's home his host found him not sleeping but praying. This consummated in his mind the mounting evidence that Francis's change was authentic and his convictions worthy to be trusted. He resolved to join Francis in a life as a penitent.

This moment rendered the first occasion when taking the vow of poverty collided with real life, for Bernardo was laden with properties in and around Assisi. He asked Francis what one should do who had received property from a master who had entrusted it to his care, and who had had possession of it for many years but now desired to keep it no longer. "What would be the best way to act in such a case?" he asked.

Francis answered, "Give it back to him of whom he had received it."

Bernardo's predicament demanded legal maneuvering. So, together he and Francis consulted another man of law in Assisi, a prominent citizen named Pietro of Catanii. Pietro's family, like Bernardo's, was well-respected among Assisi's nobility. He lived in the neighborhood of the Cathedral of San Rufino among the other nobility, including Clare's family. Pietro, like Bernardo, had been flummoxed by Francis's strange new allegiance and even more so now that the renowned Bernardo di Quintavalle had embraced the same. The three men shared many probing conversations. In turn, Pietro too joined them in their desire to embrace the penitent life. Thus, together they explored how to appropriate this new allegiance, given their current station. The three set out together to the Church of San Nicolò—next door to Francis's childhood home—where Francis knew the priest. The priest read verses from Matthew's Gospel: "If you want to be complete, go, sell what you own, and give the money to the poor. Take nothing for the journey. All who want to come after me must say no to themselves."[39]

Francis concluded this was the answer and told Pietro and Bernardo to "go and fulfill everything you have heard."

Adjustments

At this juncture, it is necessary to enjoin the reader to understand that Francis himself honored the fact that not everyone who desires to live for God receives the call to do so by adopting a vow of poverty:

> Blessed Francis also warned his brothers never to judge or criticize those who live in luxury, eat fastidiously, and indulge in superfluous and splendid clothes; God, he said, is their Lord and ours; he has the power to call them to himself and to justify them. He insisted that the friars should reverence such men as their brothers and masters and they are indeed brothers since they are children of the same Creator. . . . [H]e also said to the brothers: "Since you speak of peace, all the more so must you have it in your hearts. Let none be provoked to anger or scandal by you, but rather may they be drawn to peace and good will, to benignity and concord through your gentleness."[40]

God used people of great wealth to enable Francis to advance his work and his mission. The "vow of poverty" as it is explored in this chapter does not impugn or suggest that those whose lives are lived out of an abundance of wealth are somehow missing the mark. This chapter, to the contrary, is a touchstone for those who seek to understand the principles that render material possessions as a means to holiness.

Over the course of time Francis himself realized that the vow of poverty, as he so strictly applied it, was an untenable model for the thousands who, in his short lifetime alone, desired to embrace his form of penitence. As mentioned in the Introduction, Francis conceded as much and lent an alternative model, the Third Order, for the earnest pilgrim who longed to live the Franciscan Way but who had constraints that precluded adopting the strict dictates of the First Order.

Lessons from Involuntary Poverty

Francis had said, "the Lord is pleased with poverty and above all with poverty that is voluntary. I deem it a royal dignity and mark of nobility to follow the Lord, who, being rich, became poor for us." Yet, in all probability, many who reach this level of grace get there *involuntarily,* which God does not despise, and which was the case for me.

When I am given the opportunity to speak with suffering women whose marriages are falling apart and who come to me for advice about how to navigate the trauma of it, I have found that my response to them is simple and pragmatic. I state simply that they must fight to protect themselves financially, in whatever form, to gain spousal support. My reasons for such mundane, if seemingly unholy advice arise from my own miscalculations that carried calamitous and enduring repercussions for me. At the time when divorce became the inevitable path for my ruined marriage, and in the subsequent painful discussions, including my solicitation for spousal support, these solicitations were rebuffed, and I did not press the point. This was because I simply did not have the heart to fight this battle amid the exhaustive other battles then being waged in my life and circumstances. I would bitterly regret this posture. It brought me great suffering in ways I could not have seen.

As time passed, circumstances in my now-untethered life evolved in a way that sent me on a downward trajectory. For a variety of reasons, securing a steady income in my post-divorce years proved elusive. Writing opportunities dwindled. I began to flail financially, and the pincers of a kind of poverty began to close in on me. This altered my life in every way.

Even as I had become a champion of St. Francis, who upheld poverty as the defining feature of his devotion, for those of us—particularly women—with no safety net, there was nothing spiritually transporting about it. It was degrading. Even St. Clare, who fought till her dying day for the privilege to uphold Francis's ideal of poverty in her Order, had a stable roof over her head from which she could not be evicted. People in circumstances such as those in which I found myself do not have options and are left at the mercy of the decisions of landlords that directly affect their lives. There are few who fully grasp the mental and spiritual strain of struggling to meet one's monthly bills, the decisions that must be made, the choices that must be ascribed to. There was a time during this season of my life when I would put off doing my laundry because (at the time) to do a load of laundry would cost me $2.50, which (then) would buy a half a gallon of milk. So I would stretch the days between laundry loads, thinking, *Who will notice? It's not as if my clothes are new!* You pay for milk and eggs with saved nickels, but hesitate because, of all American currency in metals, the nickel is the only one that retains its value. (Did you know that pennies that were minted before 1982 are worth two cents? Get out your magnifying glass and start checking your pennies!)

Inevitably, when I could no longer make my rent payments, I was forced into the involuntary degradation of needing to live in temporary stints in the homes of others. Yet even in the context of such generosity of spirit of those who hosted me, these occasions felt like another layer of ignominy and diminishment. I was living by others' schedules and separated from the accoutrements that had given definition to my life. I floated between the world I had lost and the stable world of those who sheltered me. I found my world defined by layers and layers of other peoples' interests, living in a world of others' tastes in decor, other people's coffee pots. I would think about my books (then in storage), and when I spoke of them I was asked, *Why do you need your books?* You are not in your own skin. You live in someone else's skin. It is a pleasant skin, but it is not your skin. This makes it confrontational.

The discomfort is especially acute in the context of a culture that tends to interpret wealth through a type of moral equation. One person became so exasperated with my plight as to proclaim to my face, "You really don't want to get a job, do you?" If you are poor (and I apply the term loosely), some will assume that your financial predicament is self-inflicted, and you do reach a point where you stop explaining yourself.

Over time, at least for me, you feel yourself shut down. You begin to hear yourself say, *I have failed.* I remember reading a book around this time about a man who escaped from Burundi who was living in a tenement house in New York City and got lost trying to navigate the subway system. I was reading the narrative of his sorrow and struggle of feeling so disoriented and alone, on one level relating to the feeling of isolation he felt. I remember consoling myself as I read his story: *I've never seen a dog on a dusty street carrying the severed head of a man the way the man from Burundi has.* The strain of the powerlessness associated with poverty distorts one's thinking in this way. Such thoughts, for me, were not so much an expression of self-pity but more of bewilderment; I simply couldn't reckon with what had become of my once-vibrant, self-possessed life and livelihood. I would hear myself say, *So many bad people have solid incomes!*

Mother Teresa, in her poverty, wrote to her friend the Archbishop Perier: "Please pray for me, that it may please God to lift this darkness from my soul for only a few days. For sometimes the agony of desolation is so great and at the same time the longing for the Absent One so deep, that the only prayer which I can still say is—Sacred Heart of Jesus, I trust in Thee."[41] To which her devoted friend responded:

> With regard to the feeling of loneliness, of abandonment, of not being wanted, of darkness of the soul, it is a state well known by spiritual writers and directors of conscience. This is willed by God in order to attach to Him alone.[42]

So, despite my involuntary experience with poverty, which hadn't been a vow so much as a collision, I came to see that it benefitted my soul. Something happens to a human spirit when all of your safety nets are removed, when there are no tethers to keep you from bottoming out. When you have to live day to day, month to month, under the cloud of uncertainty, that does its work upon an interior landscape. The rewards of all the losses that are incurred in the struggle of poverty, whether it's voluntary or involuntary, create a refining process that clarifies and purifies. When such trials have done their work, the end result is Mother Teresa's definition of true poverty: "real and complete poverty" is "not starving—but wanting to be really dead to all that the world claims for its own."[43] Once that happens, the soul is free of the distortions and distractions of modern life.

That's not to say there won't be anxious interludes. When you don't have money and you have obligations, it's only human to experience dissonance and a degree of disquietude. That's the battle. So you're in a battle, and the battle of poverty is one that is stark and pointed, but the resultant clarity of mind and heart and soul are real and palpable and immovable. So in our exploration of the Franciscan vows, the point isn't to just make yourself poor for the sake of "being poor." There's nothing great about that. Poverty is hard and there is nothing romantic about it. But the exertion of constraint does its work, and that work is of great value. The point is to understand that such exercises of human effort in the face of the unknown are what recreate your inner being and reorder your inner landscape.

This is what St. Clare calls "a glorious exchange," as described in a letter she wrote to her protégée, Agnes of Prague. Agnes had been destined to be the queen of Bohemia and, in assuming the Franciscan vows, had literally given up a kingdom. Clare consoled her:

> [C]ontempt of the world has pleased you more than its honors; poverty more than temporal riches; and storing up treasures in heaven rather than on earth. . . . For I am sure that you know

> that the kingdom of heaven is promised and given by the Lord only to the poor, because—as long as something temporal is the object of love, the fruit of charity is lost. You know too that a person . . . cannot fight with another who is naked, because the one who has something that might be grasped is more quickly thrown to the ground. . . . It is indeed a great and praiseworthy exchange to give up the temporal for the eternal."[44]

Lessons from Voluntary Poverty

Angela of Foligno, who lived a generation after Francis and Clare, was a Third-Order Franciscan who embraced Franciscan poverty after having been born into a wealthy Italian family. She had spent the early years of her adult life seeking material wealth and worldly pleasure. She married a man of high social standing with whom she bore several children. Even so, she continued to pursue social ambition and increased wealth, even to the point of engaging in adulterous relationships. Then, at around the age of 40, she experienced a dramatic conversion, repenting of her wanton pursuits in great sorrow. Tragedy struck soon thereafter when her mother, husband, and children all died in close sequence.[45] This is the point at which she sold all her worldly possessions and joined the Third Order Franciscans, founding a lay women's religious group to serve the poor and live a life of penance and humility.

Angela was also a prolific writer, and she documented the graces she received as a result of adopting Franciscan poverty in a volume titled *The Book of Divine Consolation of the Blessed Angela of Foligno*,[46] a few highlights from which I include below:

- *Poverty produces self-reflection* because choosing a life of poverty enables a person to know oneself and to know God. What one can endure and the spirit with which one endures it expose the measure of a human soul and the power of God to sustain it.

- *Poverty offers grace* because the corner of the penitent's heart that cries out to God in utter dependence receives "grace upon grace, light upon light, and vision upon vision," and thereby comes to a more intimate and dynamic understanding of God.
- *Poverty fosters perfect humility* because such penance displays one's complete satisfaction in being "cherished in the heart of none save of God alone, and by Him alone to be held in good repute."
- *Poverty removes the tendency to judge others* because when someone has attained this level of personal devotion—of denying oneself to follow Jesus—it removes any tendency to judge others. "[He] pronounces no judgment upon any other creature whatsoever, nor seeks to judge others, as the Gospel says."

Angela's picture of the benefits of poverty can be summarized in two words: *utter dependence.*

A more contemporary writer captured the essence of Franciscan poverty without himself having taken the vows. The seventeenth-century poet John Donne wrote in a sermon about Jesus's call to the fishermen to leave their nets: "Even murmuring at poverty is a net; leave that. Leave thy superfluous desire of having the riches of this world, though they may flatter thy self . . . [Y]ou fish for a net, even that which you get proves a net to you and hinders you in the following of Christ and you are less disposed to follow him when you have got your ends. . . . [R]ich and poor are both equal, that both must leave themselves without nets, that is, without those things which, in their consciences, they knew retard the following of Christ. . . . [A]ll my life is a net, and I am bound to leave that."[47]

The Franciscan understanding of poverty departs distinctly from the human understanding of it. Francis used to tell his brothers that poverty "shone more brightly than the sun and therefore the eyes of the flesh cannot see it or function in its light."[48] When he would beg for alms, he did not see it as a degradation but as a means to open up for the giver the possibility to experience the greatest of all possible gifts, having a share in Jesus's life and being a participant in his testimony. He used to say, "To offer the love of God in exchange for alms was generosity worthy of a nobleman and anyone who thought less of it than money was a fool." Francis's poverty became the vehicle through which someone else was given an opportunity to lay hold of the love of God and the blessing of Christ. Francis gave them that, even as he joyfully begged for alms from them.

Thus, for Francis, true poverty was not a renunciation but a benediction. It meant taking action related to worldly station that is at once refining and empowering. It is refining in the sense that forsaking worldly attachments burned away the dross of self-importance. The vow is empowering in that what is left after such attachments are overthrown is a human will that is unassailable. It burns away the flesh in exchange for a robe of ineffable light. The true essence of Franciscan poverty radiates transformative force on a human soul in the same way the energy of the sun draws forth and empowers life from the earth invisibly and irreversibly.

The point of the vow of poverty is not so much about renouncing money for money's sake; it is about renouncing that part of the soul that has become distorted under a self-referring measure of one's own station. It was a practical matter for Francis. He understood that all matters of religious conviction are practical—there are no abstractions. It was a concrete call to a concrete way of living.

Poverty, for Francis and Clare, meant disqualifying themselves from the arena of wealth as the way to wield influence and control. They removed themselves and were indebted to no one. This enabled them to wield an authority that no one could challenge or undermine. They walked freely in the world "naked"—as Clare put it in her letter to Agnes—because they possessed nothing that might cause them to be thrown down. The world had no claim on them. Such a benediction was the cornerstone of Franciscan "theology of poverty." God's character is laid bare through vulnerability when his trusting children cry out before the bountiful Creator.

What would such a vow look like in today's world? How might one exact the benefit of the spirit of poverty while living the Franciscan Way? In answer to these questions I suggest that Clare would say that, in part, it would involve a glorious exchange, as noted above: "It is indeed a great and praiseworthy exchange to give up the temporal for the eternal." This implies cognition and will, an intentional act of giving up one set of priorities for another; of laying down devotion to worldly status and station and taking up higher allegiances. This might mean passing on a job promotion or forgoing the new car in order to live more simply and avoid rampant consumerism. Angela of Foligno would add that such an exchange involves an acceptance of an element of sheer dependence upon God's graces and provision. This could suggest that, for the sake of honoring God's faithfulness, we lay down avenues of power in work or status, allowing ourselves to yield to a degree of powerlessness. John Donne indicates that both rich and poor must "leave those things which, in their consciences, they knew retard the following of Christ." For all, adopting such a vow is a matter of human will and clarity of priorities. Mother Teresa perhaps sums it up best and most simply when she says that true poverty is "wanting to be really dead to all that the world claims for its own." When such a new allegiance is attained, Francis says, poverty "shines like the sun and therefore the eyes of the flesh cannot see it or function in its light." It is a mystery, in other words.

You might ask, given the value of the vow of poverty and the spirit of the vow of poverty, would I still advise women whose marriages are on the brink of collapse to petition and fight for spousal support? Yes, I would and do. Because it is often the case that women who find themselves in ruined marriages not of their making have already suffered great harm and will yet experience much more suffering. Suffering will do its work on their souls, and monetary poverty may yet lay hold of them. Francis always showed grace to the suffering, and he was vigilant before his death to make sure that Clare would be cared for. If there is no one else to care for you, I would tell these women, you must, under God, care for yourself, as this, too, is part of the Franciscan Way.

Prayer

Our Father who art in heaven—
Help me to believe this day that there is a power
to lift me up which is stronger than all the things
that hold me down. Amen.
—George Buttrick

To Ponder

Can you identify an area of your life and/or station about which the Spirit might be whispering to you, "leave that"?

Have you, in your life, made a "glorious exchange" of any kind, or have you pondered doing so?

What do you think Saint Teresa meant when she defined true poverty as a desire to be dead to all the world claims as its own?

What would be an example of the something the world claims that might still have a hold on you?

CHAPTER TWO
CHASTITY

Holy Chastity consecrates the body.

It is my soul that gives life to my body,
and it is You who give life to my soul.
—St. Augustine

As in the case of poverty, a vow of chastity involves a mystical transaction whereby a choice that is made externally carries transformative significance internally. Just as something ineffable and empowering occurs under the constraints of a kind of poverty, so too the reckoning of one's physicality affects a spiritual realignment under the appropriation of a kind of chastity.

According to the catechism of the Catholic Church, chastity is defined as "the successful integration of sexuality within the person and thus the inner unity of man in his bodily and spiritual being."[49] Its primary feature includes an incarnational aspect wherein the physicality of a person is bound to one's spiritual nature. The definition further states that "sexuality, in which man's belonging to the bodily and biological world is expressed, becomes personal and truly human when it is integrated into the relationship of one person to another, in the complete and lifelong mutual gift of a man and a woman." This suggests then that "chastity" does not of necessity mean going without sex; but it does mean the consecration of the body in whatever station to which you have been called by God, whether in marriage or in singleness. While God's earliest command to man and woman was to "be fruitful and multiply," the vow of chastity recognizes, as Francis did, the tenuous, sometimes treacherous landscape of sexuality and how a person can easily lose one's bearing, abandon constraint, and embrace destructive habits under its lower influences. Sexuality is such a primal aspect of human identity that all manner of hazards and distortions attend it, often to the ruination of souls. Understanding and appropriating a vow of chastity is the antidote to that ruination.

A Tradition of Misplaced Imagination

Struggles against lust of the flesh in the imaginations of the godly are not new to the landscape of church history. St. Augustine writes poignantly, "For my will was perverse and lust had grown from it, and when I gave in to lust habit was born, and when I did not resist the habit it became a necessity."[50] Saint Francis himself lamented to his brothers, "I lived in sin" (referring to his wild youth). Late in his life, even when he was nearing death, he exhorted them: "Don't canonize me too soon. I'm perfectly capable of fathering a child."

Augustine and Francis stand out as two among many who, having basked in lascivious and appalling pre-conversion lifestyles, overcame their lusts through self-abnegation and mortification. These two in particular carried on fruitful ministries in the name of Christ with such integrity and power that they can rightly be said to have changed the course of church history, if not the world, despite their early indiscretions.

The vow was handled by Saint Francis and Saint Clare in two distinct and contrasting ways. Francis—having been a lusty stallion in his youth and (it could be said) addicted to sex—threw himself into snow banks to quell the beast. Clare, conversely—longing for love, but renouncing it—cultivated a vivid "holy imagination," defining herself as the adorned bride of the Heavenly Spouse festooned with herbs and flowers on her breast. The disparity of these examples makes clear that appropriating chastity as a way of life is defined by the interior necessities of the individual devoted soul. In either and all cases, the body is holy. By whatever means is necessary, a desire and commitment to amplify and defend this sacred domain is what the Franciscan "vow of chastity" looks like.

Francis's Struggle

I've already noted how Francis dealt with his carnal impulses by throwing himself into snow banks to quench the fires of lust:

> [The devil] prepared a different [temptation], namely, an urge of the flesh. . . . The devil sent into him a violent temptation to lust, but as soon as the blessed father felt it, he took off his clothes . . . saying: "Come on, Brother Ass, the tunic belongs to religion: no stealing allowed! If you want to leave, leave!". . . However, when he saw that the temptation did not leave even after the discipline . . . he opened the cell, went out to the garden, and threw himself naked into the deep snow.[51]

He imposed rigorous disciplines on his brotherhood, understanding the need both for external constraint and internal resolve in order to battle and overcome fleshly forces that assault the spirit. He and his clerics faithfully recited the Daily Office of devotion—liturgical readings at regular points of the day and night.[52] (See the Glossary.) He ordered them to fast and confess and serve and discipline one another, to do penance, to absolve, and to work with their hands to avoid idleness. Equanimity in office; outer rigors of communal accountability; inner disciplines of rhythmic praying, fasting, meditating, and solitude; constant confessing; yielding to rebuke; and ultimately shattering mercy enabled this passionate troubadour and his brotherhood to walk the line between fleshly weakness and holy estate.

In a way, it could be said that this is what "incarnational theology" looks like. God's saving activity is shown in taking on flesh as the point of contact through which he showed himself to humanity and through which he mounted their rescue. Flesh and blood were the vehicles through which he righted and reclaimed intimate habitation among a downward-leaning human race.

Jesus said that whoever loves his life will lose it and whoever hates his life will keep it. Paul said, "I'm all right with weaknesses, insults, disasters, harassments, and stressful situations for the sake of Christ."[53] He said, "I bear the marks of Jesus on my body."[54] Perhaps the most powerful "incarnational" words uttered from the mouth of the Lord for his followers, which carry the same power today, are these: "This is my body, given for you."

G. K. Chesterton describes God coming in flesh and those of the flesh trying to appropriate God's nature through the flesh as part of the paradox of faith: "[W]e want not an amalgam or compromise, but both things at the top of their energy; . . . both burning, . . . both things at once and both things thoroughly."[55]

Francis knew well the weakness of the flesh. He also knew the temptations of ecclesial office, woefully evidenced in the corrupt state of the medieval church. He therefore ordered the brothers "in whatever places they may be among other people to serve or to labor, not to be . . . overseers in the houses in which they are serving; nor are they to accept any office that may give rise to scandal or bring about the loss of one's soul. Rather, let them be inferior, subject to all who are in the same house."

As I've said, we cannot all take the Franciscan vows. At the same time neither can we alter the language and traditions of the medieval church that conceded certain kinds of renunciations as the means of achieving intimate acquaintance with God. But one can, and indeed must, appreciate the paradox. God himself chose human flesh to bring amnesty to his fallen race. Such terms imbue "the flesh" with beauty and dignity and purity in all its passions. But humans are weak. Enthusiasms of flesh can easily degenerate to "cold sensuality, a sodden and filthy spiritual wretchedness," to borrow from Dorothy Sayers. Men and women need reminding of their weakness, before God and one another, in order to stand strong against the "heady wine" of misplaced imagination such as defined Francis's early years.

Clare's Longing

Clare's approach to channeling the natural impulses of love showed itself in the then-widespread form of devotion known as "bridal mysticism."[56] Many female contemplatives embraced bridal mysticism, also known as "love mysticism," to answer the natural feminine longings they had renounced upon joining a penitential religious order. Feminine spirituality resonated with the penitential movement in the Middle Ages, since many women joined the movement as means of freeing themselves of the obligations and constraints of rank and class and, in so doing, forfeited marriage and having a family.

Drawn from imagery in the Song of Songs, these mystics experienced their relationship with God as a love affair of the soul in spirit and a betrothal to Christ as divine husband, which Clare expressed vividly in her letters to Agnes of Prague. Agnes was a woman of royal rank who renounced her heritage to join Clare's Order in a life of poverty. Agnes was the Abbess of the Poor Clares in Prague, and Clare wrote her many letters, four of which survive. In these surviving letters, Clare calls Agnes a "spouse and mother and sister of the Lord Jesus Christ" and assures her that "the King himself will take you into the heavenly bridal chamber." She advises Agnes to "look into the mirror" and see in her face the bejeweled spouse of the Divine Husband. She is a bride festooned with adornments of her beloved: "He has adorned your breast with precious stones and placed his priceless pearls on your ears." Clare says that since such desire is planted into the human heart by God, this true unmet longing is a desire for the experience of God himself. The bride rises and meets her Holy Groom, who crowns her with precious stones and places "blossoms of springtime on [her] head, a golden crown as a sign of holiness."

I have encountered objections from some in evangelical circles that dissent from the kind of feminine spirituality that highlights a vision of God that echoes romantic language. Yet a close look at the motivation and influences of bridal spirituality suggests that the objections of these friends are misplaced. The spiritual exertions that define this brand of devotion are intended to elevate one's mind and will, seeking to rise to higher levels of intimacy and sanctity. The first indicator of true love, according bridal mysticism, shows itself in "forsaking all others and taking only him unto herself."[57] The women who embraced this spiritual vision abandoned all forms of self-gratification save those that embodied true devotion to the Beloved Spouse. They left the world, forsaking all others (as Clare and Agnes did), incurring the world's contempt while embracing a life of humility that such a choice inevitably requires. But this is the way of life of their Beloved Spouse, and it is in his footsteps they follow.

Beyond a willingness to forsake the praise of the world, another property of such devotion is "to *be transformed* in the properties [or attributes] of the Beloved." These properties show themselves in, first, possessing a love of all creatures, which reflect God's creativity and originality; second, being humble and gentle, which Jesus modeled in his interactions with outcasts, the rejected, and castoffs, and even his own disciples; and, third, showing oneself to be steadfast—the will always to be moving forward, claiming each step for the love of the Spouse. ("For the nearer the soul is to God, the less it changes in its own self."[58])

The meaning here is simply that by inner discipline and exertions of the mind and heart, the devoted follower of the Beloved Husband can assume the traits that reflect his nature. These attributes reflect Jesus's own way of interacting with those in his world. Bridal Mysticism marks these exertions as the way for the "bride" to show her devotion to her Lord. "Keep control over yourselves and give not yourselves to any creature, neither lend yourselves whatsoever; but give yourselves wholly to Him who says, 'Thou shalt love the Lord with all thine heart, and with all thy mind, and with all thy soul, and with all the strength that thou hast.'"[59]

This complete transformation of the bride can be likened to Jesus's description of what it takes to enter the kingdom:

"The kingdom of heaven is like a merchant in search of fine pearls. When he found one very precious pearl, he went and sold all that he owned and bought it."[60] There is only one pearl: It is of inestimable value, and to attain it requires all. This is the essence of bridal mysticism, the inner journey which, over the years, won Clare's allegiance and defined her devotion. So while the accoutrements of this faith expression might be alien to the evangelical mindset (thus provoking the ire of those mentioned earlier), the essence of it lends needed granularity to the evangelical assertion, noted by my critic, that "God is commanding sinners to repent" and that "the gospel calls for repentance and faith."

These aspects of Clare's brand of feminism stand in stark contrast to the ethos of the modern women's movement. Rather than measure one's standing in power and position, Clare exchanged that for the freedom that comes with identifying with the lowly. Rather than execute her vocation by confrontation and grievance, Clare advanced her call with humility, charity, respect, and gentility. Rather than blur the edges of the picture of what it means to be a woman, Clare sharpened and enhanced that picture, embracing her feminine attributes without equivocation, celebrating and empowering them as festooned as the bride of Christ himself. Being a woman, for Clare, is glorious, dignified, and sanctified. She saw power in it. Though Clare herself did not experience marriage and childbearing, she embraced the validity of the unique attributes of a woman's station in that role, and more, she pondered it. Her vision of womanhood became the hallmark of her spiritual devotion and the lodestar of her chastity: She was Christ's beloved. Clare not only celebrated her womanhood in its most beautiful conception, but she also set her mind upon it and vested her very identity in that picture.

For Francis and Clare, though they understood that there are aspects of "the flesh" that are banal and subject to lower appetites, they also understood that the flesh is also integrally linked to the state of our souls and imbued with sacred possibility.

The flesh, after all, was the means through which our Savior "came to his own people."[61] As his beloved creatures who are pinned to earth—and thus fall prey to destructive forces—they (and we) have been given the gift to rise beyond those limiting forces and take hold of that holy place of grace. They understood that the flesh can *serve us*, in other words. It can be our friend, our partner on the journey. Even Francis, who because of the fleshly impulses that often plagued him his whole life, ridiculed his flesh, calling his body "Brother Ass," near the end of his life repented of this degradation. He came to recognize that his body, broken though it was, lent him mortality and carried him along the path of life, enabling him to fulfill God's purpose. At the end of his life, he thanked his physical being, no longer with the disdain of "Brother Ass" but with the dignity and affection due to "Brother Body."

A Theology of the Body

When it comes to the delicate and mysterious topic of chastity, of all the elements that comprise human personhood within the context of the Franciscan Way, this is the most personal and intimate and therefore carries the greatest potential both for sanctity and calamity. In the case of troubled marriages, as was the case in my own, the physicality of the marriage bond carries the same set of intimate possibilities for either sanctity of the bond or calamity to its ruination. This is the hidden mystery of the sacred institution of marriage. When the holiness of the station is subsumed by destructive cycles and patterns, great harm is done to one's personhood spiritually and in many other ways.

I found a passage in Dante Alighieri's poem *Il Paradiso* that helps me articulate what I mean. In the opening lines, he conveys his understanding of the nature of God's presence in the world:

> The glory of the All-Mover
> Penetrates through the universe and reglows

In one part more and in another part less.
(*Paradiso,* Canto I, 1–3)

Dante is saying that the power and the glory of God penetrate all corners of the created world, rising up and out of earthly agents that "reglow" his glory. The word in Italian Dante used for reglowing is *risplende,* the manifestation of God's strength, beauty, and power in intersection with the carnality of earth. Another volume of Dante's poetry, related to *Il Paradiso,* is *L'Inferno,* his poem on hell. In this poem he sees a similar type of divine penetration, but in reverse. In Dante's hell, the forces of darkness likewise have the ability to penetrate all corners of the created realm in a fashion similar to the forces of light as manifested in *risplende.* I call this negative penetration *displende,* mimicking Dante's habit of creating his own vocabulary when attempting to describe a thing that had no existing term of expression. Just as divine light, in *risplende*, reglows up and out, in *displende* a trajectory of darkness goes down and down to the very bowels of hell. In both instances, there is a movement of power and an inevitable spilling forth of that power—one upward, the other downward—through human agency. In one case, the movement rises toward light, while in the case of the other it is driven toward darkness and death.

Dante is trying to communicate in both poems that invisible energy penetrates the visible (the physical) world. Such energy must go somewhere. In the case of marriage, when all is in order under God's holy purpose, the beauty of God is strangely "reglowed" through the intimate physical bond. However, if the holiness of the marital estate has for whatever reasons turned dark, invisible forces still penetrate, but now in the direction of harm rather than sanctity. Again, such energy must go somewhere. If a marriage is forged or otherwise locked in destructive patterns, the unfortunate result is *displende* and the ruination of human souls.

This means that the sacred consecration of the body, which defines the virtue of chastity, can be violated in misshaped marriages. Christian marriage is an invisible and mystical force. If it is played out according to godly prescriptions, it is intended to fulfill a grand design for marriage in Christ, "sanctification . . . a profound mystery." Yet when the theological force of this profound mystery applies itself in the opposite direction, the end ultimately is the opposite of sanctification and becomes more likened to an extinguishing.

In the context of a marriage—and I speak now as one who has wrestled with this issue in my own marriage—these matters carry highest import, because the hidden work of these invisible forces sets a course that moves a soul in one direction or another, toward light or toward darkness.

As one considers the vow of chastity in this world where the physical realm is at once glorified and distorted, accentuated, and in many situations ruined, taking such a vow means understanding the sanctity of one's physical being and making decisions in accordance with that sanctity that defend and protect one's physical domain. Such decisions could fall under issues related to sexuality, or other destructive habits such as drug or alcohol abuse. There are any number of possible avenues through which the physical realm might be stifled as a conduit to "reglow" the glory of God.

The Scottish fantasy writer George MacDonald wrote that "it is through the body that we receive all lessons of passion, of suffering, of love, of beauty, of science. It is through *the body* that we are both trained outward from ourselves and driven inward into our deepest selves to find God. There is glory and might in this vital evanescence, this slow glacier-like flow of clothing and revealing matter, this ever uptossed rainbow of tangible humanity."[62] Perhaps if we consider the nature of chastity as consecrating our bodies and rendering them the honor they are due, we can sanctify our time in this world and imagine our lives as MacDonald's uptossed rainbow. Clare wrote to Agnes to "look into the mirror" to see in her face the bejeweled spouse of the Divine Husband. Perhaps we too can summon a picture in our minds so as to see our place in these beautiful realms. When we die—as we all will—we might then have a share in the lucidity Clare expressed when, with her dying breath and despite the many losses of her life, she said, "God, you are blessed because you have made me."

Prayer

I come, O Lord, unto Thy sanctuary
to see the life and food of my soul.
As I hope in Thee, O Lord, inspire me with
that confidence which brings me to
Thy holy mountain.
—Clare of Assisi

To Ponder

Have you experienced a collision or intersection between your life in the flesh and God's holiness? What does it look like? Have you made any decisions that directly affect the physical side of your holy being?

Do you agree with the notion that, if sin becomes entangled in a holy estate (such as marriage), the sacred power of that estate will work out negatively, affecting a downward spiral that the author calls *displende*?

CHAPTER THREE
OBEDIENCE

Holy Obedience consecrates the heart.

Obedience is so excellent a virtue
that our Lord wished to direct
the whole course of His life by it.
—Francis de Sales

Of the three overarching Franciscan vows, the vow of obedience lends the greatest challenge, especially for one desiring to live the Franciscan Way but who has no formal affiliation with a religious Order or perhaps even a church. Even if one is an active member of a worshipping body, generally speaking there is no official apparatus whereby a lay member "comes under obedience" of a church leader. (This is especially true of the Protestant tradition.)

The concept of obedience is confusing for many since over the centuries of church history it has taken on differing forms and applied in diverse ways. In the early church well into the Middle Ages and even today, the penitential movements within Christianity required that vows be taken by those desiring to embrace these reforming impulses. To follow Francis of Assisi in the thirteenth century required that the novice embrace not only the vows of poverty and chastity, but also a vow of obedience. Francis himself took those vows upon the occasion of the renunciation of his life and rank as part of Assisi's rising merchant class. Clare took the same vows when she left her childhood home and noble rank to follow Francis. For them, the vows did not express a negative rejection of privilege so much as they manifested a positive gesture of consecration.

As the concept evolved, it became a signature spiritual discipline that was operational even for everyday Christians who desired spiritual direction amid their secular lives. The sixteenth-century spiritual writer Saint Francis de Sales took many interested learners under his tutelage and taught them the layperson's guide to the vow of obedience. He considered such a guide "a heaven-sent angel" who will "put into his heart and mouth that which is needful to you so that you ought to hearken as though he were an angel come down from heaven to lead you thither."[63]

Francis de Sales was insistent that holy obedience can be cultivated in any context in the course of a person's everyday life; a person does not need to be part of a religious Order to gain access to the benefit of such obedience. Aspiring to a holy life does not in any way suggest an abandonment of one's "regular" life or vocation. To the contrary, cultivating such devotion beautifies everyday work and makes pure and joyful even the most mundane existences. The practice must be adapted according to one's vocation and station, according to de Sales, because it would be wrong to misappropriate one's exercises in a way that contradicts one's calling. "It is an error, nay more, a very heresy to seek to banish the devout life from the soldier's guardroom, the mechanic's workshop, the prince's court, or the domestic hearth. . . . [T]rue devotion does better still, for it not only hinders no manner of vocation or duty but, contrariwise, it adorns and beautifies all."[64]

Under Francis of Assisi's model of obedience, his followers (as already noted) were required to adopt strict standards and mortifications, prayers, and daily duties. The measure of their devotion was evidenced in their willingness to obey such strictures and make such concessions. Francis himself came under obedience on a variety of occasions amid the vicissitudes of his growing and changing order. For example, at the Chapter meeting of all the Franciscan brothers that convened in May of 1220 shortly after Francis's return from Damietta, Egypt, the Order initiated some critical decisions that made it clear to all that the movement had outgrown Francis's ability to manage it. (More than five thousand friars at that point numbered among their ranks.) To maintain stability under its staggering growth, Francis himself enjoined his friend the bishop of Ostia, Ugolino, to become the Order's official guardian and to shepherd it through this tenuous time. The following fall, in September 1220, at the gathering held on the Feast of Saint Michael, Francis stepped down as vicar, citing declining health, appointing his friend Peter Catanii as his replacement: "From now on I am dead to you. Here is Brother Pietro di Cataneo, whom I and all of you shall obey."[65]

Clare was challenged by the vow of obedience when Francis asked her to assume the role of abbess (like a "house mother") of the female followers who had amassed at the small abbey of San Damiano. This meant that Clare would be the initial abbess of the female Order of Franciscans, then known as the Second Order. She strongly objected to assuming the role. She did not want to be an abbess with the authority, obligations, and constraints that attended the role: "They granted and withdrew benefices, took part in councils and called synods; in many dual cloisters *they* exercised authority. Often, like the abbot, they had the jurisdiction of a bishop without full powers of consecration. This meant that they exercised temporal and spiritual power in their realm just as the bishop did in his diocese. The liturgical sources and rites of consecration show that abbesses often received the staff and miter and thus full teaching and jurisdictional authority."[66]

Sister Pacifica di Guelfuccio, who was a childhood friend of Clare's and who joined her at San Damiano, testified during the investigation for the process of canonization shortly after Clare's death, and described the intensity of her resistance: "[T]hree years after Lady Clare had been in the Order, at the prayers and insistence of Saint Francis, who almost forced her, she accepted the direction and government of the sisters."[67]

Clare had had other ideas about how she had hoped to live out her religious life. But she was under obedience—the third of the threefold vows she had willingly assumed when she left her family home to follow Francis in the life of "a religious." After that, her life took turns she could not have imagined and would not have preferred. She had wanted to be itinerant in the same way that Francis traveled hither and yon. She had aspired even to martyrdom in the effort to share her message with the Saracens. Despite these noble and heartfelt impulses, she honored the vow she had taken to live under obedience.

Yet how can such a vow be truly realized in the life of one who does not have the benefit of a structure of religious life such as is found in belonging to a religious order?

The Principles of the Garden

The principles of a vow of obedience, for me, came into sharp relief in my side vocation as a flower farmer. Perhaps the clarity of high principles being faithfully exemplified in the work of a farmer explains why so much of Jesus's teaching about the Kingdom of God arises from stories related to agriculture:

> "A farmer went out to scatter his seed. As he was scattering it, some fell on the path where it was crushed, and the birds in the sky came and ate it. Other seed fell on rock. As it grew, it dried up because it had no moisture. Other seed fell among thorny plants. The thorns grew with the plants and choked them. Still other seed landed on good soil. When it grew, it produced one hundred times more grain than was scattered." As he said this, he called out, "Everyone who has ears should pay attention."
>
> His disciples asked him what this parable meant. He said, "You have been given the mysteries of God's kingdom, but these mysteries come to everyone else in parables so that when they see, they can't see, and when they hear, they can't understand.

> "The parable means this: The seed is God's word. The seed on the path are those who hear, but then the devil comes and steals the word from their hearts so that they won't believe and be saved. The seed on the rock are those who receive the word joyfully when they hear it, but they have no root. They believe for a while but fall away when they are tempted. As for the seed that fell among thorny plants, these are the ones who, as they go about their lives, are choked by the concerns, riches, and pleasures of life, and their fruit never matures. The seed that fell on good soil are those who hear the word and commit themselves to it with a good and upright heart. Through their resolve, they bear fruit." (Luke 8:5–15)

This simple picture describes the complexities of seed cultivation, revealing the principle that, for a garden to thrive, all the necessary preparatory steps must be executed. There are no shortcuts. Care of the seed, soil, and manifold other contingencies must be exerted faithfully and consistently for the harvest to come to fruition and render nourishment. The disciplines of tending a garden must be met devotedly at every stage. Any slippage in the upkeep could forfeit the crop. This is how cultivating a garden exemplifies the exercise of obedience. Gardens grow in their own time, and the gardener must submit to that timeframe; a garden will not speed things up or slow things down to service the gardener's personal preference.

Yet amid the rigors of garden upkeep, from the moment I place the first small seed into a sea of dirt, I am participating in a miracle—the act of putting seeds in dirt and then watching life rise out of it is the picture of the fruit of obedience. And not life only, but life upon life. The process of co-creation, one miracle at a time, does not cease. The fruits of the earth keep giving generously and extravagantly. It is no wonder Jesus anchored so many of his teachings about God in the ways of nature. Being a participant in the miracle of the garden is healing to the soul and is grounding because, for this bounty to grow and thrive, it must be tended. Tending a garden takes you outside of yourself because if it is not tended, it will die. You will lose the miracle. If you tend it under obedience it gives extravagantly. Sometimes ruined soil must be torn up before true growth can happen. But—another miracle!—once torn up, even the most stubborn earth can be coaxed into vibrancy and sustainability.

In the same way and in the most minuscule expressions, I have found, as a gardener, that tending the garden has also tended to my soul, day to day and row by row, even as the plants are clipped, the soil amended, the bouquets arranged. In attempting to appropriate the vow of obedience into my life, I would bear in mind the lessons of the garden. The mission of the gardener means *planning your garden.* The same could be said of discerning your spiritual journey. What do you want your life (spiritual and materially) to look like as you live the Franciscan Way? What will you embrace? What will you give up? Then it involves planting the appropriate seeds and tending your seedlings—do they have enough water, heat, and sunlight? It means weeding them—extracting the negative toxins that might otherwise overtake the vulnerable seedling. Then pruning comes in—that is, cutting back undisciplined and unwieldy growth that impedes the robust advancement of the mission. Then harvesting the fruit, winnowing the chaff, and bringing the garden to rest when the season is concluded mark the final stages of obedience in tending a garden. During dormancy, the soil recovers and regains nourishment for seasons yet to come.

Just as the reward of applying such principles renders a vibrant, abundant, and robust garden, so the benefit of the principle of obedience can render a healthy and robust interior disposition. The will and fortitude of the farmer meets the providence and sustenance of God. "Trees bear fruit only because of the presence of the sun, some sooner, some later, some every year, and others every three years, not all of them always yielding equal harvests," Francis de Sales wrote. He likened the work of the sun upon the tree to the operations of God upon our souls. "We are very fortunate to be able to remain in the presence of God; so let us be content that he will make us bear fruit sooner or later, every day or only occasionally, according to his good pleasure to which we should be fully resigned."[68] The obedience of the farmer and the operations of the sun create something heretofore nonexistent but which has assumed the fullness and beauty and promise of heaven itself.

Yet not all spiritual sojourners are farmers and gardeners. Neither do they have access to flowers and fields to train one's mind and shape one's will in the application of obedience. How then can such a vow be realized?

Prayer

The principles of the garden, cast upon a wider screen, have already been noted: soil preparation, planting, watering, weeding, pruning, harvesting, and so on. Thus, it is required of one who seeks to grow in devotion to determine his or her metaphorical "field" to which one renders such obedience. In other words, find your gift, your mission, your vocation under God and for the purpose of his Kingdom and the benefit of your soul, and give yourself to that purpose in the same way a farmer devotes his every effort to keeping his field growing.

Perhaps it is helpful to consider that the beginning point of the vow of obedience for the lay person is prayer. The distinguished spiritual writer Peter Kreeft reminds us: "Prayer is our obedience to God even when it asks God for things, for God *commanded* us to ask (Mt 7:7)."[69] There are three reasons that we are commanded to pray, he says. "Prayer gives truth to our mind, goodness to our will and beauty to our heart."[70]

> Prayer gives truth to our mind because it puts us in the presence of Truth itself . . . . It gives goodness to our will because [it puts us in position to] catch the good infection of Godliness by contact . . . [and] it gives beauty to our heart because it plunges us into the heart of God, which is the eternal energy of infinite joy.[71]

Prayer, in other words, is the starting point for performing the operations of the garden upon the soul. It clears the field of toxins and readies it to receive seeds of new possibility; it does the needed continual work of pulling out the weeds of sin and habit that compete with new life, and it cuts back disproportionate growth of bad habits and inclinations. This, in the end, brings forth a harvest of truth, goodness, and beauty. Kreeft himself likens prayer to the work of the gardener: "Praying is like gardening: the growing of something alive—in this case alive for eternity. It is gradual and it is invisible, but it is the difference between life and death."[72] The gardening theme is likewise echoed by St. Francis de Sales: "We must make two equally firm resolutions: one, to be ready to see weeds growing in our garden; the other, to have the courage to see them pulled up, and to pull them up ourselves."[73] I have often prayed a special prayer when sensing the need for such purifying work upon my soul:

> O Holy Ghost, my Lord and my God . . .
> I am nothing and can do nothing without You.
> Come, blessed Spirit of God, and dwell in this soul
> that longs to be your holy temple.
> Heal the lurking distemper of my heart
> and infuse your grace into the wellsprings of my life.[74]

Holy Friendships

A close proximity to establishing a model of obedience might also be realized in the bond established in the context of spiritual direction. Thomas Merton, in his book *Spiritual Direction and Meditation*,[75] describes the relationship this way:

> [W]e must not make the mistake of thinking that direction is a luxury reserved for the special elite. For if, as Eric Gill said, "every man is a special kind of artist," it is perhaps true that every man has a special and even perilous vocation to complete the supreme work of art which is his sanctification . . . . A spiritual director is, then, one who helps another to recognize and to follow the inspirations of grace in his life, in order to arrive at the end to which God is leading him.[76]

In the year following my divorce, I put myself under the watch care of a spiritual director, and the stabilizing effect of this bond was palpable. I wrote in my journal at the time: "I slept peacefully last night—the first time in weeks—because, having now been 'tethered' to a director, I felt like I couldn't fall; I had been hanging on the face of a cliff, slipping, scraping, hanging by bloody fingertips, and my director came and secured ropes and clips about me, anchoring me so that, while I was still on the face of the cliff, I am secure; I can't fall. I don't have to depend on myself or fear my incapabilities to make this climb. I still must make it, but with the aid of another weight counterbalancing mine, with the companionship of one who speaks life into me, with the knowledge that, if my foot slips and I miss a foothold, the ropes will hold."

The director is one, says Merton, "who sympathizes, who makes allowances, who understands circumstances, who is not in a hurry, who is patiently and humbly waiting for indications of God's action in a soul. . . . [T]he director is interested in our very self, in all its uniqueness, its pitiable misery and its breathtaking greatness."[77]

De Sales urged his friend Madame Louise de Charmoisy, wife of an ambassador of the Duke of Savoy, to pray for the right guide for spiritual direction. "So, daughter, inasmuch as it concerns you so closely to set forth on this devout journey under good guidance," he wrote to her, "do pray most earnestly to God to supply you with a guide after His Own Heart, and never doubt but that He will grant you one who is wise and faithful, even should He send you an Angel from heaven."[78] "A faithful friend is the medicine of life," he wrote, "a storehouse of wisdom to us in our sorrows, trials and falls; he will be as a healing balm to stay and soothe our heart in the time of spiritual sickness; he will shield us from evil and confirm that which is good in us; and when we fall through infirmity, he will avert the deadly natures of the evil and raise us up again."[79]

A Personal Rule

Before moving on from the Franciscan vows to turn our thoughts to the virtues, there is one more tool that might assist the seeking pilgrim in his or her journey toward an interior reordering. This would be to write a personal Rule. Each branch of Francis's Order (the First Order, the Second Order, and the Third Order) possesses a Rule, or governing document. This document is a lodestar to guide the actions and comportment of the individuals who've put themselves under obedience to that respective Order. When I was visiting Assisi, shortly after that initial trip that launched my journey along the Franciscan Way, in my reading I began to latch onto some seminal principles that forged my sense of purpose moving forward. In turn—and in keeping with the model of St. Francis—I wrote a personal rule, which has likewise served for over two decades as a lodestar for me amid the vicissitudes of life.[80] "A tree bears its fruit in silence," Thomas Merton said. It grows both downward and upward, its roots farther into the earth and its branches higher up to the sky. The reach of the tree's uppermost branches depends fully upon the depth and health of its roots. Roots are invisible, so the human eye cannot see the power that is derived through them nor the engine-like energy they exude constantly that results in the growth of the tree. It is helpful for me to think of the life of obedience in this way. That is, the most significant and life-producing aspect of our spiritual health is hidden from sight, sometimes even from our own sight, but is constantly, slowly, and invisibly feeding us in a way that produces a higher reach and a stronger constitution. For our part, our obedience is to keep the soil nourished and the roots watered, which is the little bit we can do to allow the mighty, invisible, and silent force of hidden growth and holy fruit to work its magic through us.

Living by prayer or coming under the guidance of a "heaven-sent angel" does not, of necessity, execute the needed devotion that shows itself in obedience. Ultimately, appropriating such a vow resides in the will of the one assuming it. Even as a novice seeking to join an Order submits to an overseer, he or she does so by an act of will and has the ability to desist at any time. So bringing to bear this holy vow in the circumstances of your life will stand or fall on the exertion of personal will before God. That is why coming under a vow of obedience "is an act of great humility."[81] It "puts to rout all self-centered and carnal desires and keeps the body subject to the obedience of the inner person and to obedience to one's brother or sister."[82]

With that thought in mind, it seems appropriate to shift our gaze from exploring the imposition of the vows and ponder the exercise of virtues, starting with the virtue of humility.

Prayer

O most high, glorious God,
enlighten the darkness of my heart
and give me right faith, a certain hope and a perfect love,
understanding and knowledge,
O Lord, that I may carry out your holy and true command.
Amen.
—Francis of Assisi

To Ponder

Thinking of the landscape of your life, your call, and your vocation, in what ways might your prayer life undertake the needed "soil cultivation," "planting of seeds," "watering" and "pruning"? What might your "harvest" look like?

Have you ever considered fashioning a personal rule as an early step in training your will in the discipline of obedience? If so, what elements might it include?

Part Three

VIRTUES

INTRODUCTION TO THE VIRTUES

One should not say that it is impossible to reach a virtuous life;
but one should say that it is not easy.
Nor do those who have reached it find it easy to maintain.
—St. Antony of the Desert

If the vows are imposed from the top down, the virtues are borne as fruits of the thirsting soul arising organically from the ground up. Pursuit of virtue echoes a sentiment expressed by the apostle Peter: "have your minds ready for action. . . . [Y]ou must be holy in every aspect of your lives, just as the one who called you is holy."[83]

The great medieval spiritual writer Thomas à Kempis wrote of the challenge of pursuing virtue: "When a man stands upon himself he is easily drawn aside after human comforts. But a true lover of Christ, and a diligent pursuer of virtue, does not hunt after comforts, nor seek such sensible sweetnesses, but is rather willing to bear strong trials and hard labors for Christ."[84]

The exercise of the virtues, alas, is often driven by soul struggle: occasions of injustice, betrayal, effrontery, ingratitude. It is in the context of such moments that we are challenged to give entrance to the exercise of virtue. Otherwise such soul-stretching moments would not be considered virtue!

Not too long ago I purchased a "kitty" for the purpose of rendering some form of companionship in my later years (as cats tend to be known for, hence, "cat people"). She's a Maine Coon, a breed known to get fairly large and to take on the relational attributes of a dog. When I received her, she was a diminutive fairy-creature with wide eyes and splaying ears, fleet and light as the air. Yet, at the same time, there was a bit of a monster in her. She gnarled and clawed at perfectly lovely things—things I cared about, like special pillows and my Italian bedspread. She tore at them as if on a mission to destroy (there's no other way of putting it). My arms, legs, even my face at points were bloodied by her irrepressible pouncing and leaping. At times, she would latch on even to me without warning—as if climbing a tree—albeit with affection but to deleterious effect. The consolation I sought from my dainty kitty cat in the early days did not pan out. Instead, I felt like I was in the company of a monster, sweet, lovely, and dainty though she may be.

One of the most vexing aspects of having this young kitty, however, was her inexplicable and neurotic need to jump on tables, desks, and shelves (anything high up) and start tapping with her paw any items resting there, moving them this way and that until the ritual ultimately culminated in the final push off the surface. Whatever it was that she was fixated upon would come crashing to the floor. This chaos added to my already exasperating habit of dropping things myself—to the extent that the smallest gesture, such as pulling a notebook from a shelf, inevitably meant inadvertently dropping the item placed next to the notebook and then, when leaning down to pick up the dropped item, snagging my sweater on the corner of a chair and then knocking over the coffee mug trying to free my sweater. All this while simply trying to slide a notebook from its shelf. I came to consider dropping things part of the exercise of the virtue of patience.

Perhaps my new kitty's purposefully knocking things off my tables with willful intent was the Holy Spirit sent to me, reminding me that circumstances will abound in life that upend the little bit of "order" I convince myself I am managing. And, more to the point, such order is a mere kitten's paw away from utter demolition. In a similar way, unforeseeable circumstances will arise that will throw into chaos moments or situations we otherwise thought would be "under control." Such moments challenge us to maintain a measured and upright bearing rather than capitulate to a visceral riposte. This is the arena where the exercise of the virtues arises.

Yet, too, there also are those treasured moments when my little furry friend curls about me, snuggles near me, and, rather than ravaging my environment with her claws and teeth, instead simply confers the gentle purring that so defines the companionship of a cat. Sometimes she will lick my face with affection, and the Spirit will remind me that there is a place for a spirit of gentility and consolation, too, in the Holy Spirit's graces, despite the demolitions. My kitty is always near, though she sometimes completely upends my so-called ordered world, and sometimes she carries the weight of it.

Aspiring to attain the virtues is a little bit like taming a kitten. There is beauty, purity, possibility, and gentility, but there is also barbarity, a clawing of an untamed beast. There will be pain, but also there will be the graces of a fleet-footed fairy spirit that awakens the early moments of a new day and lends warmth to the chill of gray Novembers. In the end, one day (I see it now), that trouncing, pouncing menace of a kitty will become fully grown, settled, self-possessed, and majestic. That is the picture of the spiritual work of growing in virtue.

St. Francis sang the praise of Holy Virtues in his "Salutation of the Virtues":

> O all you most holy Virtues, may the Lord save you all. . . .
> each puts to rout vices and sins.
> Holy Wisdom confounds Satan and his wicked ways.
> Holy Simplicity confounds the wisdom of the world and the flesh.
> Holy Humility confounds pride
> and all the people in this world
> and in like manner all things that are in the world.
> Holy Charity confounds all temptations that come from the devil or from the flesh, and all human fears.
> Holy Poverty confounds cupidity and avarice and the worldly cares.
> Holy Obedience puts to rout all self-centered and carnal desires and keeps the body subject to the obedience of the inner person and to obedience to one's brother or sister.[85]

Whereas the final two virtues listed above are already examined under the Vows in Part Two of this volume, the chapters included in Part Three explore the other four virtues noted in Francis's salutation (though there are more). Francis de Sales highlights a few additional virtues in his exhortation: "Let us practice . . . those lowly virtues to the attainment of which our Lord had bidden us labor—I mean patience, cheerfulness, self-mortification, humility, . . . kindness to our neighbor, forbearance toward his failings, diligence and a holy fervor."[86] While this exploration highlights only four, one can hope that, once gainfully striven for or otherwise attained, additional benefits of varied virtues might naturally be born.

CHAPTER FOUR
HUMILITY

Holy Humility confounds pride.

In order to receive God's grace in our hearts,
they be as empty vessels—not filled with self-esteem.[87]
—Francis de Sales

St. Francis understood humility to be the exercise of human spirit that gives entrance to the surprising movements of God. Unlike the vows, Francis did not *impose* humility as a precondition to following him or joining his Order. In the Franciscan Way, the virtue of humility would become the natural outworking of obedience—putting oneself "under" a greater authority—regardless of any personal effrontery such a posture might elicit. When he was granted permission to establish his Order, Francis insisted that they call themselves "friars minor" (lesser brothers) because they were to remain "very humble with regard to all the men of this world, humble in all their behavior and by their example as well as by their name."[88] Later, when the Order had been firmly established and Pope Gregory IX asked Francis if some brothers might be promoted to offices in the church, Francis answered, "My lord, my friars are called 'minors' so that they will never think of becoming superiors. If you want them to bear fruit in the Church, keep them strictly to their vocation and never let them take any office in the Church."[89] His biographer Thomas of Celano, in his second work, wrote of him:

This prince of God
could not be identified as a prelate,
except by this sparkling gem:
he was the least among the lesser.[90]

Humility is the Antidote to Pride

Of the carnival of unfriendly forces that afflict a person arousing all manner of interior disruption—personal offense, agitation, aggravation—the antidote to them all is the exercise of humility. *Yes* (you might hear yourself say), *that person is being a jerk.* And, *How can anyone abide such a jerk?* In such a moment, the whisper of the holy virtue of humility arises in your mind and you hear a rebuke: *Oh, yes, he is indeed a jerk; you are quite right, even as you yourself have blindly exhibited your own version of it to the affront of others. So the jerk you see in him touches you because it strikes the chord of that jerk that is in you.*

Humility requires a pause, then, in the face of personal effrontery. It is that pause that is the "exercise of human spirit" (noted above) that allows entrance to the surprising and rehabilitating movements of God. In that liminal space the Spirit of God gains entrance and does its necessary work on an aggravated soul. This work is the holy reminder about who we ourselves are at our core and that left to primordial impulses we claim high ranking among the jerks. It is only the movement of God that neutralizes such tendencies and frees us to rise higher, to become more clearheaded about such realities, and, in turn, to be calm, patient, even sorrowful of our own sin in the presence of others' "jerk-dom."

This side of humility is the antidote to pride, which is the tendency in every human heart to assume, if unwittingly, a position of rank over another. Pride assumes the posture of "looking down"; you're higher up and so better able to see the faults of those below you. Francis's biographer Bonaventure said, "The saint had a horror of pride which is the cause of all evil."[91]

Humility is the Antidote to Fear

It is similarly necessary to address another side of the exercise of humility that does not arise from pride so much as from fear. For some, it is not difficult to be ever mindful of one's own contemptible nature. It echoes in their heads. How many times have you said to yourself, *You idiot!* This can be the default vernacular, particularly of those who have been victims of emotional or other forms of abuse. Such abuse survivors naturally buckle in spirit and assume a posture of belittling their own value and showing little compassion for their own failings. There may be hesitancy or unwillingness to step into a larger conversation for fear of one's own inadequacy or of being rejected. This crippling predisposition can likewise be met, healed, and empowered under the proper exercise of the virtue of holy humility. It takes much humility for a person of great gifting who has been summoned to lay it aside, to freely do so. Equally, it takes the same measure of humility for a person of great gifting who has been summoned to serve under that gifting but who feels inadequate to do so, to take up the mantle anyway and rightly serve. For the one, ingrained pride and a false sense of self-importance must be cast aside, while for the other, ingrained fears and insecurity must be overthrown. Proper humility is the answer to both.

Francis himself in his pre-conversion life was consumed with vanity and bravado and personal abandon. He was an untamed stallion. His natural ways were destined to become his undoing. Yet, as is often the case for larger-than-life personalities, life intervened and put his mind in proper proportion. His nature was greatly tested and tempered by the calamities that befell him at various points in his early life. His grandiose but failed flourishes to gain knighthood, his romantic idealizing of courtly love and his sexual prowess, his vanities about setting fashion trends from France—every feature that defined his early life was upended when he found himself in the prime of his youth languishing in a squalid prison cell. The "gift" of humility was hard won for Francis. But in the end, it became a signature feature of his post-conversion life.

On one occasion, in a telling episode, Brother Masseo asked Francis a question that has proven to be the defining theme of his movement: "Why after you? Why after you? Why after you? Why does all the world seem to be running after you and everyone seems to want to see you and hear you and obey you? You are not a handsome man. You do not have great learning or wisdom. You are not a nobleman."

In answer to Brother Masseo Francis responded: "You want to know why after me? You want to know why after me? I have the all-holy eyes of God that see the good and the evil everywhere. For those blessed and all-holy eyes have not seen among sinners anyone more vile or insufficient than I am. And so in order to do that wonderful work which he intends to do, he did not find on earth a viler creature and therefore he chose me. For God has chosen the base things of the world and the despised to bring to naught the noble and great and strong."[92]

As noted in Part One, the episode where Francis embraced the leper utterly transformed him personally, but the episode likewise reflects the way in which Francis's movement turned upside down the operating principles of the established Church in his day. His embrace of the leper and the resultant complete transformation meant for Francis and his movement that the leper, once the lowest of the low and outcast by all, was now front and center in his understanding of "hierarchy." I note in my biography that Francis's vision of the gospel turned the prevailing social order governed by the Church on its head. For some, Francis's identity with the social fringe could have been seen as tantamount to a call to revolution against the Church. Yet in truth, the only revolt Francis had in mind was the invitation to bring the outcast in from the edges and place him front and center in the family of God.[93]

Francis's humility meant that he rendered honor to the outcasts. This was borne out in an episode the brothers faced relating to a gnarly and ungrateful leper. It demonstrates the depth with which his humility commanded his life. As recounted in one of the early biographies:

Now it happened once in a place near the one where Saint Francis was then living, that the friars were taking care of leprosy patients and sick people in a hospital. And a certain man was there who was so seriously ill with leprosy and so impatient and irritable that everyone was sure he was possessed by an evil spirit. For he attacked any of the friars who nursed him with horribly foul language and shot insults at them like arrows, but what was worse he would also whip and wound them in various ways. Yet the most fearful and worst of all was that he would curse and blaspheme the Blessed Christ. No one could be found who could or would take care of him. The Friars therefore decided to abandon that man completely in order not to become blasphemers of God and supporters of an instrument of the devil.

But they did not want to do this until they had duly told the whole story to Saint Francis. After hearing them, Saint Francis went to that perverse man and, entering, greeted him: "God give you peace, my dear brother."

The man answered reproachfully: "What peace can I have from God who has taken from me all peace and everything that is good, and has made me all rotten and stinking?"

Saint Francis said: "My dear son, be patient, because the weaknesses of the body are given to us in this world by God for the salvation of soul. So they are of great merit when they are borne patiently."

The sick man replied: "How can I bear patiently this constant pain that is afflicting me day and night? For not only am I burned

> and crucified by my sickness, but I am sorely wronged by the friars whom you gave me to take care of me, because there is not one who serves me the way he should."
>
> Francis said, "Dear son, I want to take care of you, since you are not satisfied with the others."
>
> The sick man replied, "All right. But what more can you do for me than the others?"
>
> Francis said, "I will do whatever you want."
>
> The leprosy patient said, "I want you to wash me all over because I smell so bad that I cannot stand it myself."
>
> Francis immediately had water boiled with many sweet-scented herbs. Next, he undressed the man with leprosy and began to wash him."[94]

Clare's Tonsure

As for Clare, the first mark of her humility was evidenced in initial ritual of initiation into Francis's fellowship of followers when he cut her hair. That gesture, known as the tonsure, is a dramatic and decisive consecration both for male and female penitents, signaling their intention to "leave their lives in the world and embrace a new kind of life under a different set of rules."[95] (See the Glossary.) For Clare, the gesture carried additional significance in that her beauty was the stand-out feature of her maidenhood and her hair was its crown. (Tresses of her hair remain on display to this day in the reliquary at the Basilica of Santa Chiara in Assisi.) Medieval professor and Franciscan historian Marco Bartoli notes that Clare was not an ordinary young girl leaving her parents to enter monastic life, nor was Francis a bishop—to whom the consecration of virgins was normally reserved. "In fact," he says, "he was not even a priest but only a layman, and yet he took upon himself the right to consecrate Clare."

Clare had not undergone a novitiate, so the tonsure at the hands of Francis would not have served to make her a nun. "Clare promised to observe no rule, she did not receive a monastic veil, she did not enter any settled, canonically erected community. . . . [T]he tonsure before the altar of Saint Mary of the Porziuncula was not a monastic consecration but a penitential gesture. Clare did not become a nun but a penitent, a *mulier religiosa,* a religious woman, a woman of penance."[96]

Aspects of her self-identity—both the one of nobility she left behind and of the new one of poverty she was now forging—were marked with humility, abandoning a life of privilege as a marriageable noblewoman in exchange for becoming, essentially, a beggar in beggar's clothing.

Francis Makes Her Abbess

Even at this early stage, more women were joining Clare at San Damiano and others were establishing small female monasteries in nearby locales. Francis's following was likewise swelling to surprising numbers, and he began to recognize the need to bring order to the chaos. Francis was an astonishing figure in many ways, but one way he was not astonishing was as an administrator. Inevitably, when the numbers increased, the Order's operations had to be managed. And managing things was not Francis's forte either. I've already described in the previous chapter how, as part of his effort to harness the growth of his unwieldy movement, he enjoined his partner Clare to take charge of the women and bring the community at San Damiano under a greater discipline. To that end, he asked her to assume the role of abbess—something Clare very much did not want to do.

The role of the abbess in the Middle Ages was one of power, and, as I noted in the previous chapter, the idea of wielding such power repulsed Clare and she fiercely resisted Francis's request. She relented, under obedience. Since obedience demanded her acquiescence, thereafter, humility became her lodestar. Even in this elevated role, Clare eschewed the authority of power that attended it. She forged her role as abbess as more pastoral than judicial. In her *Form of Life* (1253) she described the role of the abbess as one who is chosen by the sisters (and not appointed by those higher up) and as one who "strive[s] to preside over the others more by her virtue and holy behavior than by her office, so that, moved by her example, the sisters may obey her more out of love than out of fear."[97] Her life itself was the picture of humility, the image of a maiden who had swept away the vanities of her vaunted and lofty claim to nobility in exchange for the picture of a beggar. This upside-down image of the woman who once claimed the rank of Assisi's town beauty and most coveted bride, through the sheer force of the graces bestowed upon her through her exercise of humility, rendered for her not only more actual power in her lowly role, but an echo of that power that has resounded through the ages and that is perceivable still today, for those with ears to hear it.

The occasions when this holy attribute will be called upon to be exercised by the growing Christian will be painful. I can offer a personal experience as a case in point. I found myself on the outer edges of a situation of a very serious, potentially tragic circumstance related to a much-loved member of my extended family. Without going into specifics, I can go as far as to say that, despite standing from a vantage point somewhat at a distance, I felt a deep sense of duty to open a conversation with this relative and share some information that might offer options for a way forward out of this potential tragedy. Given the tenuous nature of this particular predicament, I hesitated, not wanting to insert an opinion that might cause further confusion or upset. I pondered my actions this way: I could keep my peace and withhold the information which (I thought) could bring hope, or I could broach the subject gently, with humility, in the hope that a wider conversation might result and good will realized. In the end, constrained by the hope of possible deliverance from this near-tragedy, I opted for the latter and reached out accordingly.

My instincts proved wrong. My relative did not receive or appreciate my gesture. On the contrary, she rebuked me. I apologized, as I rightly ought to have, and stepped away from further engagement. This moment proved a testing field for a proper exercise of humility. In my rumination following this painful episode, I pondered greatly where, in the exercise of humility, is a line rightly to be drawn when a human life dangled in the balance and (so I reckoned) the information I imparted could potentially restore that life. As it happened, help or no, and hope or no, the information was unwanted. Conferring it didn't help. I was wrong to have conveyed it. Thus I pondered still more—would I have been a better Christian to have withheld such sentiments simply to "live and let live" (or die), as the case may be? The answer, actually, may be "yes" to that dilemma, but this remains a conundrum in my mind.

I felt great sorrow for the additional angst my words brought to the already distressing situation, and I rebuked myself. Not only did I rebuke myself, but I also carried the weight of this self-rebuke in a painful and sustained way for a period of time in the aftermath. Thus, in time, I found myself pondering yet another set of lines that must be drawn. At what point, I pondered, do I a draw a line around these self-recriminations? How far do I allow the downward spiral of these afflicting thoughts to take me? At what point do I put a halt to it, forgive myself, and move on?

I was comforted by the words of St. Francis de Sales, who said, "Prepare your heart to be at peace, then take great care throughout the day to call it back to that peace frequently. . . . Say to your soul, 'There, we have made a mistake, but let's go on now and be more careful.' When you are rightly accused of some fault, humble yourself very much and acknowledge that you deserve the accusation brought against you. . . . If, after your genuine and legitimate excuse, they continue to accuse you, do not be at all troubled and do nothing to get your excuse accepted. For doing your duty to truth, you ought also to do it to humility."[98]

So the balance to strike when cloaking oneself in proper humility is to find the place of truth and stand upon it, measured against the graces of humility. Whether you are in the right or in the wrong, in hard moments it is your duty simply to bear it and acknowledge it. Beyond that, even if there may be a measure of reproof that must be borne, insofar as you have faced personal failings with honesty and clarity, move on. If recriminations follow, rightly or wrongly, keep going without any further defense or self-recriminations.

The mistake often made by some who ponder the virtue of humility is to think it is shown strictly in self-deprecation and perhaps even a degree of self-loathing. Francis himself often publicly announced his failings in grandiose assertions accentuating the loathsome nature of his early sins. He carried this testimony around like a burden on his back and, near the end of his life, he forgave himself and grew to understand and even be grateful for the course his life had taken. Yet because of the lavish, unharnessed nature of his pre-conversion sinful extravagance, for many years he reproached himself in a way that seemed disproportionate, especially in the light of the blessedness his life exhibited once he surrendered in obedience to become the new man God was creating out of the old man.

There is a place for an intimate acquaintance with one's own sinfulness. Ancient philosophers asserted the maxim "know thyself," while St. Paul called such self-knowledge "sober judgment, in accordance with the faith God has distributed to each of you" (Rom. 12:3, NIV). Sober judgment and true self-knowledge require an honest assessment of our own wretchedness and misery. But "sober judgment" requires that this assessment be tempered with higher thoughts. True humility, says Francis de Sales, also requires an appreciation for "the excellence and dignity of our souls, which are capable of being united to Divinity by His infinite goodness. It does not consist only in mistrust of ourselves but also in confidence of God."[99]

Many persons have deceived themselves by a false and foolish humility, which prevents them from looking at the real good that God has implanted in them. Worse than that, such false humility presumes to suggest that God made a mistake or somehow got it wrong. Such judgment is abhorrent before God. For the gifts that God has bestowed on each of us ought to be recognized, esteemed, and highly honored.

My friend Frederica Mathewes-Green wrote that "God puts others in our lives not only for our joy and comfort but also to irritate and provoke us, so that our flaws rise to the surface where we can recognize them and deal with them."[100] She adds, "People have different ideas of what 'love' should look like. What onlookers see a holy person doing might not always fit their definition of the word. But it will indisputably look like humility."[101]

By way of an addendum to the sad episode wherein the virtue of humility was exercised painfully upon me, the relative I had upset lost the loved one whose life had hung in the balance. A part of me carried some trepidation at seeing this relative, for the first time since our uncomfortable exchange, when I attended the funeral. I feared that my misstep would carry lingering distress. To the contrary, this grieving family member embraced me warmly, and all residual effects of my mistake evaporated in the presence of grief and familial affection. Perhaps the proper exercise of humility in the critical moment opened the way for these higher graces to prevail. Who knows? Proportionate, measured, and true humility renders an interior ballast to all involved that enables generosity of spirit.

So the virtue of humility is an odd and perplexing mix of pain and reward. De Sales likens the paradox of this virtue to the operations of the bee: "Watch a bee hovering over the mountain thyme; the juices it gathers are bitter, but the bee turns them all to honey. . . . So also the virtues practiced in the bitterness of the most vile, low, and mean trials and humiliations are the most excellent of all."[102] Ultimately, despite the pain and seeming degradation, the spirit of humility becomes sweeter than honey, and those who nourish themselves with this honey produce sweet fruit.

Prayer

Keep me, too, and so your gifts will grow and reach perfection
and I shall be with you myself,
for I should not even exist if it were not by your gift.
—St. Augustine

To Ponder

When you consider the virtue of humility, do you see it more as an antidote to your pride or as an antidote to your fear?

Where would you see yourself when making a "sober judgment" of yourself in the exercise of humility? Do you need to be kinder to yourself, or would a dose of self-reproach benefit your soul?

CHAPTER FIVE
CHARITY

Holy Charity confounds all temptations that come from the devil or from the flesh and all human fears.

If I fail grace, it will also fail me.
—Francis de Sales

The previous chapter concluded with the thought that the virtues of humility and generosity are inextricably linked, and that the one carries the mirror image of the other. When Francis de Sales says that "humility and generosity are so closely united to one another that they are and never can be separated,"[103] his understanding of generosity captures the meaning I bring to the virtue of charity—open-handed grace and largesse of spirit. In this chapter I juxtapose the terms *generosity* and *charity* as if they were one and the same.

In his desire to impart to his students an understanding of charity, de Sales urges them to draw a distinction between "the higher part of our soul and the lower."[104] The latter is rife with doubts and confusion and is often swayed by visceral impulses. (This region of the soul is where most of us dwell most of the timc, alas.) Charity "banishes by its presence all the little follies and softnesses that serve only to hinder us on our way," he writes.[105] The charitable soul, in other words, "pays no heed to such considerations and simply sets itself to work to fulfill this charge without saying a single word."[106]

Of the four virtues explored in this offering, the most difficult for me personally is the exercise of charity. The virtue of charity carries layers of meaning and redounds in benevolent possibility. Yet, for those who, like me, at times succumb to the lower reaches of the soul and *want justice*, the exercise of charity can be at best counter-intuitive. When I think of those who have done me wrong, other reckonings come to mind. I would like them to see a light that shows them their sins and to repent with weeping and beg for forgiveness.

Such thoughts are alien to the one who exerts the obligations of the virtue of charity. The generous soul would, instead, plead God's mercy on these broken souls even as one pleads God's mercy on one's own broken soul, asking for healing in their blindness and praying them into the glorious kingdom of grace—and not praying only, but extending the hand that escorts them there.

So many slights and betrayals come our way in the course of a lifetime and in the course of a day. This will always be so, because, in the end, despite best intentions, self-preservation often prevails in the actions of men and women, sometimes even over religious devotion or if it means betraying a trust or higher obligation. It is the rare soul who will be true to honor and duty if it requires the sacrifice of one's station or well-being. So, to constantly clamor for justice is a hard road to walk. Your one and only blessed and holy life will be reduced to only that: clamoring. It is beauty you want, grace-filled, holy, and unflappable. So when the betrayals come, when the slights poke at your sense of self-importance, and when you are affronted by insults, be ready to deem these as gifts that will train you in the virtue of charity.

Charity in the end frees you from the most onerous burden we carry: the ball-and-chain of "self." Our poor wretched "self" will wrestle us to the ground if we give it that power. Let's find a way out from under it. "Self," on one level, matters only insofar as our beloved Savior took upon himself the task of redeeming the very concept of self by imbuing each personality with eternal possibility and a new life. So, in that regard, the "self" matters wholly and deeply.

Yet, where "self" must otherwise be tempered is when, in its grip, it demands just deserts—fist waving and all that. There is so much that has gone so wrong for so many in every walk of life that if we all abandoned ourselves to going around waving a fist in the cry for justice there would be nothing left to define human existence other than people waving indignant fists at every other human *ad infinitum* into eternity.

The glory of holy charity is that it frees us from the impulse of just deserts, and in freeing us individually, bit by bit, it frees the world. Grace enters into the otherwise bleak human story, finding that sacred space where a human soul can relinquish the ever tormented and tormenting "self" in deference to the possibility of a new spirit. Only when virtue is exercised and the lower habitations of self-will are subjugated to the higher relinquishments, can this new magnanimous spirit of charity arise supernaturally.

At the same time, justice, in its true sense, is not jettisoned in the practice of the virtue of charity—nor should it be. The meting out of justice is simply transferred to the proper queue for an appropriate accounting by the One (and only One) who is able to rightly divide such lofty and nuanced reckonings. Nor does exercising charity nullify the actual harm that results from another's ill-treatment. To the contrary, a true exercise of charity is anchored in truth, and that truth will and must stand. This means that if harm has been done, that harm stands, along with the attendant consequences. Damage incurred from betrayals or abuse is not overridden in the exercise of charity. Yet, in the soul of one who seeks it, charity can rise, even in the context of such damage. It can find a way forward, leading ultimately to the healing of one's own damaged soul.

The exercise of charity empowers true liberation as the broken and distorted "self" gives way to largesse. This creates a new possibility for a suffering soul. It opens the way for holiness. Francis de Sales said, "There is only one true devotion while there is a very large number of false and meaningless ones."[107] Charity is the mark of that one true devotion. This is attested by the Apostle Paul and many others after him: "though I have all faith, so that I could remove mountains, and have not charity, I am nothing. . . . And now abideth faith, hope, charity, these three, but the greatest of these is charity" (1 Cor. 13:2,13, KJV).[108]

When Francis Exhibited Charity

For St. Francis, amid the struggles associated with his life and embrace of poverty, the spirit of charity consistently defined his life and interactions with all whom he encountered. Charity was primal to his understanding of Christian devotion.

One such instance when Francis defined charity as a seminal virtue involved a very painful and difficult passage. He wrote a heart-wrenching letter to "a minister" sometime between early 1221 and 1223.[109] This minister had been put in charge of the unwieldy Order by Francis himself and had raised concerns to him about opposition, possible harm, and even mortal sin. The minister suggested to Francis that he was contemplating, instead, the desire to retreat to a hermitage. In response Francis wrote:

> To Brother [N.] minister, May the Lord bless you.
>
> I speak to you as best I can about the state of your soul. Consider as grace all that impedes you from loving the Lord God and whoever has become an impediment to you, whether brothers or others, even if they lay hands on you. And may you want it to be this way and not otherwise. And let this be for you the true obedience of the Lord God and my true obedience, for I know with certitude that it is true obedience. And love those who do those things to you and do not wish anything different from them unless it is something the Lord God shall have given you. Love them in this and do not wish that they be better Christians. And let this be more than a hermitage for you.
>
> And if you have this, I wish to know in this way if you love the Lord and me, his servant and yours: that there is not any brother in the world who has sinned—however much he could have

> sinned—who, after he has looked into your eyes, would ever depart without your mercy, if he is looking for mercy. And if he were not looking for mercy, you would ask him if he wants mercy. And if he would sin a thousand times before your eyes, love him more than me so that you may draw him to the Lord; and always be merciful with brothers such these.[110]

For Francis, spiritual aspirations were never mere abstractions; they always showed themselves in concrete gestures in everyday life. This is seen further in another lovely intimate moment, noted in *The Mirror of Perfection*, that renders a glimpse into Francis's generous heart.

> While he was staying at Saint Mary of the Portiuncula, a poor old woman who had two sons in religion, came to that place seeking some alms of the blessed Francis because that year she did not have enough to live.
>
> Blessed Francis said to Brother Peter [Catanii], who was the general minister at the time, "Have we anything to give our mother?" For he used to say that the mother of any brother was his own, and that of all the brothers in the religion. Brother Peter told him: "We do not have anything in the house that we can give her, especially since she wants such alms as would provide for her corporal needs. In the church we only have one New Testament for reading the lessons at matins."
>
> Blessed Francis responded, "Give our mother the New Testament, so she can sell it for her needs. I firmly believe that the Lord and the Blessed Virgin, his Mother, will be pleased more

> by giving it to her than if you read in it." And he gave it to her.[111]

Showing a spirit of charity was so elemental to Francis and his understanding of conduct of his Order that it was woven into the essence of the Rule (governing document) he adopted for the Friars Minor near the end of his life. In the Order's Rule of Life in 1223 he wrote that when a brother was put in the position to correct a wayward brother, that he was to do so "humbly and charitably, without commanding them anything that is against their conscience or our Rule." "With all my heart," he added, "I beg the friars in our Lord Jesus Christ to be on their guard against pride, boasting, envy, and greed, against the cares and anxieties of this world, against detraction and complaining, [that] they should realize instead that the only thing they should desire is to have the spirit of God at work within them, while they pray to him unceasingly with a heart free from self-interest."

Clare's natural predisposition toward charity fit naturally into the role she would assume as the first female follower of Francis and later as abbess. Yet even before she left her family home as a young girl, she embodied this virtue in her actions. Despite her family of origin having been numbered among Assisi's wealthiest and their home being one of the largest, Clare often took food from the family table and put it aside to distribute to the poor. She also is known to have sold her inheritance to give it away to the poor, and she sold part of her sister's too!

In my way of seeing it, one of the most poignant and telling moments when Clare reflected the essence of truest charity was at the end of her life. It is important to remember that, despite the honors conferred upon her in memory, throughout her life as a penitent she experienced great hardship and personal struggle. Her days were filled with trials and setbacks, and she was known to have cried a lot.[112] Around the time of Francis's death, when Clare was in her mid-thirties, she had developed a debilitating affliction that took away her ability to walk, to the extent that, even as Francis lay dying, she was unable to go to him to say a final goodbye. From the prime of her life to the point of her death when she was over 60, she labored to accomplish the slightest undertaking and depended utterly upon the good will of those around her to help her get through simple tasks day by day. This physical malady was only one of many hardships and calamities that would define her days.[113]

Near the point of her death, however, it seemed as if the pieces of her wearying life converged, and, by grace, she saw herself for who she was in the eyes of God. One of the sisters, named Philippa, who was with Clare during her final days, heard her begin to mutter, and when another sister asked her who she was speaking to, Clare answered, "I am speaking to my soul." Some of her words were spoken too softly for the sisters to recount. At another point, one sister was directed to commit to memory the words Clare spoke. Near the end, another sister, Sister Benvenuta, described a vision they witnessed in Clare's room:

> A multitude of virgins dressed in white, with golden crowns, silently entered the room through the half-closed door and took up the whole room. The brightness was such that every corner of the house was inundated with it. One of the most beautiful of all, wearing a crown greater and brighter than any of the others, came forward. She went to the bed and there she stretched over Clare a veil so thin that it covered her without hiding her. The she bent down and put her face near that of the dying woman. And with that the vision disappeared and the room was again in shadow.[114]

Clare's last known words, on August 11, 1253, were uttered to herself: "Go securely and in peace, my blessed soul, for you have a good escort for your journey. For he who created you made you holy, has loved you tenderly as a mother her child. And you, Lord, are blessed because you have created me."

Clare's heart of charity found its ultimate expression as extended to her own soul. In her earlier reflections about the hidden world of the beloved bride of the Most High King, she lived only in the shadow of hope of such hidden glory. Her entire life could be understood as an exertion under that hope. In the moment of her death, that glory rose as the sun, and the virtue of charity she had always extended to others throughout her days showed itself in a singular assertion of generosity to herself. No longer cloaked in mystery and cleaving to hidden hope, but in real time and complete lucidity, she saw herself as she truly was, the way we all are summoned to see one another in the exercise of charity. She stepped into the world that she had seen only in dreams and glimmers. And most pointedly, she saw herself as the one who she had always been, the one God had always seen in her, even amidst her most desolate sorrows.

Concluding Reflections

It must be acknowledged that it is not always feasible to bring the virtue of charity into some circumstances, at least in the immediate sense. In Victor Hugo's masterpiece, *Les Misérables,* the Bishop Myriel rescued his house guest, Jean Valjean, after he had been caught stealing silverware from the rectory that sheltered him. At the point when Valjean had been caught and taken by authorities, the bishop intervened, insisting that the items had been freely given to Valjean and that he had, in fact, forgotten the candlesticks that the bishop then pressed into Valjean's hands. Now that Valjean was freed from the threat of imprisonment, the bishop exhorted him that his soul had been purchased for God and that the money from the silver candlesticks should be used to make an honest man of himself. This moment of grace saved the soul of Valjean, as the spellbinding plot of the story reveals.

Perhaps not all of us would have responded with the same charity as did the bishop, and indeed, there are circumstances that might militate against such magnanimity in real time. There are any number of crimes and violations in the face of which charity could be misguided. So I want to be clear that exercising the virtue of charity does not mean giving a blanket pass to the wrongdoing of those who do harm. But when the occasion calls for it and the offense is so grievous that the gesture cannot be immediately summoned, there is another tack to take to find a way forward toward charity. In these moments, *time* is an integral element in finding that path. Perhaps there is someone who has done great harm, whether in the immediate moment or over the span of months or years, and it is evident that there is no quick fix. Charity can nevertheless be cultivated. In such instances, the ground can be laid for charity to arise in the disposition of the violated simply by holding. By that I mean, taking a pause, rendering no gesture, positive or negative, staking no claim or responding in any way. Sometimes the sacred pause is the most powerful and holy gesture one can summon in such a moment. Such a pause allows the entrance of time to do its work. And time, in the operations of God, is not benign. It is God's tool, and he uses it. As described by the anonymous contemplative author of the compelling narrative *The Cloud of Unknowing*, "Nothing is more precious than time. In one small particle of time, little as it is, heaven can be won and lost. This is a sign that time is precious: God, who is the giver of time, never gives two particles of time together, but one after the other."[115]

If we hold the situation in holy tension before God's throne in faith he will step into the moment and imbue it with needed adjustments so that the fruit of charity can be born. Sometimes the purest and truest form of charity is realized only after the passage of time.

The nineteenth-century theologian John Henry Newman said that faith without charity "is dry, harsh and sapless; it has nothing sweet, engaging, winning, soothing. . . . It is eternal charity which is the bond of all things in heaven and earth. It is charity wherein the Father and the Son are one in the unity of the Spirit, by which the angels in heaven are one, all saints are one with God, by which the Church is one upon the earth."[116] Beyond that, as Francis de Sales says, "Charity never takes possession of the heart without bringing in her train all other virtues. But she does not call them forth suddenly, all at once, nor in all times and places. The good man is like a tree planted by the water-side that will bring forth its fruit in due season, because when a soul is watered with charity, it brings forth good works seasonably and with discretion."[117]

So, in time, the exercise of charity brings along with it all other virtues. These other virtues, in turn, bring about good works with discretion. Such discretion is most notable in the virtue of simplicity. And the virtue of simplicity, as it is reflective of God's nature, is most poignantly revealed in a person whose ministry has carried an immeasurable impact on the hearts of generations of children. I had the privilege to know and visit and write about him. His name is Mister "Fred" Rogers. He is the embodiment of the gift and power of the virtue of simplicity, which is explored in the following chapter.

Prayer

O Lord, who has mercy upon all,
take away from me my sins,
and mercifully kindle in me the fire of Your Holy Spirit.
Take away from me the heart of stone,
and give me a heart of flesh,
a heart to love and adore You,
a heart to delight in You,
to follow and to enjoy You,
for Christ's sake. Amen.

—Ambrose of Milan,
Penitential Prayer[118]

To Ponder

Has there been an occasion in your life when you might have exercised the virtue of charity, but instead understood the necessity of a "holy pause"?

Conversely, can you recall an occasion when the Holy Spirit enabled you to exercise charity when lower impulses might otherwise have gained sway? If so, can you describe the kinds of graces that resulted from this gesture?

CHAPTER SIX
SIMPLICITY

Holy Simplicity confounds the wisdom of the world.

Jesus spoke simple words.
Yet they shook the world, and still shake it.
—George Buttrick

On the day years ago when I visited Fred Rogers in his office and studio in Pittsburgh, he had been working on the concept of "big" and "little." This assignment for the magazine I worked for at the time had been my reward after spending many long, sad months researching and reporting on the tragic school shooting at Columbine High School.[119] I had requested doing the Rogers assignment, making the case that I (and the world) needed some good news to ponder. Thankfully, my boss saw the point and rendered me the assignment, not being sure himself what Mister Rogers could lend to the larger cultural conversation, but trusting that I would find out.

Most people were not aware that Fred Rogers and his "neighborhood" were the outworking of a profound sense of mission. He was an ordained minister who was commissioned under that mantle to be an evangelist working with children and families through mass media. His vision of God and his understanding of holiness imbued every aspect of the wildly successful television program *Mister Rogers' Neighborhood.*

I introduce this visit in the context of Franciscan virtues because the light that was lent by Fred Rogers in his presentation of "the Neighborhood" created the kind of clarity of standing that embodies the spiritual quality of simplicity. Fred understood that the world is complicated and filled with contradictions and uncertainties that can frighten and alarm young children. His neighborhood mimicked the simple truth that there is something higher, deeper, calmer and nearer to God than the capriciousness of a confused and frenetic world. He took his young television neighbors there, to that safe space, during his television visits, and, as a result, he conferred on generations of souls the clarity and security of the truth of simplicity. I myself experienced it the day I visited him in the Neighborhood.

That day, he was pondering the attributes of "big" and "little" and how best to communicate them in a way that his young television audience could understand.

His "office" was a small, cramped, eclectic room that he had made into a testament to the people who had "loved him into existence" (as he put it). His work space was a well-worn couch—he had no desk—and he sat there while I sat across from him in a velveteen chair. Both the couch and the chair had come from his childhood home in Latrobe, Pennsylvania, and it was from this couch that he wrote letters to children and their mothers, and it was there that he was pondering "big" and "little." He was flanked by stuffed animals and baseball caps (and sometimes stuffed animals wearing baseball caps) that his many neighbors had given him over the years.

He showed me a sign that he kept on the table near the door: *Freddie, I like you just the way you are.* "It was my Grandfather McFeely who said such things as that," he said. "We used to visit him in the country almost every Sunday. He was the kind of person who would say, 'You know, you've made this a special day by being here.'"

Then he opened his wallet to show me pictures. The "tour through the wallet" included photographs of people he'd known, children of the people he'd known, and, in some instances, people he didn't know but had heard about and cared about. "I love to know about people," he said. Turning back to the wallet: "Did you know Henri Nouwen? Here he is with Chris de Vinck," he said, explaining that Chris de Vinck was compiling a book of essays about Henri Nouwen. "These are Chris de Vinck's children."

"This is one of my special friends, Yo-Yo Ma, who is a cellist, and his son," he said. "He's a great man. Oh. This is Jonathan Kozol—he writes about children." There was a picture of Mother Martha and "some of the kids in the Bronx"; a little boy from his church; and another boy with autism who was fixated on hangers. There was a picture of a woman whose husband "was sucked into coal slag and suffocated," along with a picture of her two children.

"That's Chef Brockett." Then he paused momentarily at the next picture. "Oh, that's what I was looking for: here is Dr. Orr, and Mrs. Orr."

He proceeded to tell me that when he was in seminary he studied systematic theology with Dr. William F. Orr and that he took every course Dr. Orr offered; "He was a great influence on many of our lives. Not just because he was brilliant. He was the kind of person who would go out on a winter's day for lunch and come back without his overcoat.

"Every Sunday my wife and I used to go to the nursing home to visit him. One Sunday we had just sung 'A Mighty Fortress Is Our God,' and I was full of this one verse. I said, 'Dr. Orr, we just sang this hymn and I've got to ask you about part of it.

"'You know where it says—*The prince of darkness grim, we tremble not for him. For, lo, his doom is sure . . . one little word will fell him*? Dr. Orr, what is that one thing that would wipe out evil?'

"He said, 'Evil simply disintegrates in the presence of forgiveness. When you look with accusing eyes at your neighbor, that is what evil would want, because the more the Accuser'—which, of course, is the word *Satan* in Hebrew—'can spread the accusing spirit, the greater evil spreads.' Dr. Orr said, 'On the other hand, if you can look with the eyes of the Advocate on your neighbor, those are the eyes of Jesus.' I've never forgotten that."

In the context of our exploration of the virtue of simplicity, I believe that what Fred was saying here, in the light of his conversation with Dr. Orr, is that amid the eviscerating assaults of evil upon all that is good, pure, and true, the word of power that arises from Jesus himself that shatters the powers of darkness was exhibited during the last moments of Jesus's life when he was near death, and, despite continued harassments, he asked his Father to forgive his executioners. This simple word confounded the harassing forces of the evil one, according to Dr. Orr, and lifted the blinding fog, settled the roiling sea, and returned the ship to its tranquil harbor. In keeping with the metaphor, the rudder, then, fixed its course, and the ship sailed on and stayed true to its course. This is the power of the virtue of simplicity. (We will see it exhibited by Jesus yet again near the end of his life.) The point is, forgiveness settles the storm, and the resultant calm settles the soul, enabling a person to resume course and to advance in one's singular purpose.

"Sometimes evil is almost palpable, and we see it trying to make people sad and mad and distrustful," Fred Rogers said to me. "I think the Accuser would have us be so despairing that we wouldn't do anything good at all. But you know the effect of one little candlelight in great darkness. That sounds simple, but it's true.

"What our society gives us is shallow and complicated," he said. "But life is deep and simple. Life isn't cheap. It is the greatest mystery, and we all only have one life to live on earth."

It's Not Complicated

When I ponder the virtue of simplicity, I am helped in considering another critical moment in the final hours of the life of our Lord when his close companion turned against him and opened the path that would lead to the bitter and tortured end to Jesus's life. In the moment of fellowship around the table during his "last supper," Jesus understood the heart of his betrayer, and rather than writhe in personal effrontery, he privately pulled Judas aside and bid him to get on with it. Then, when the troops came to the garden later in the pre-dawn hours, Jesus openly approached his betrayer as if to extend one last opportunity for a change of heart. Instead, Judas greeted him with a kiss. Rather than wave a fist and call down fire on him, Jesus simply asked, friend to friend, "You betray me with a kiss?" On he went, calmly, in the exertion of simplicity, keeping to the task that his Father had given him.

Facing betrayal of any sort, whether leading to death as Jesus's did, or leading to the breakdown of a relationship, as I myself have experienced, lends decisive clarity as to the measure of one's willingness to claim the promise of the virtues. I have faced personal betrayals of those whom I trusted and loved and can attest that these moments press against the outer reaches of Christian devotion. One is fully justified in carrying outrage and anger, thrashings of mind, shock and sorrow. The disturbed situation of personal betrayal preys upon all of these emotions. Thoughts of ultimatums come to mind, of ways to punish or rebuke the betrayer. These responses are natural. But they are also visceral. And, in cultivating the virtues, and in particular the virtue of simplicity, the aspiration is to find a landing spot within one's mind and heart that is not driven by the natural—a spot where a soul can rise above the visceral in deference to the simple. This requires a supernatural grace. This is why, when the virtue of simplicity is attained, the soul exudes a sweet aroma.

In what way does one cultivate this virtue? The virtue of simplicity bids the sorrowing soul to stay the course and not give thought to what one ought "to do" in the face of betrayal. One ought to do what one has been doing and is called to do without missing a step or configuring an alternative plan. One ought not turn to the right or to the left, in other words. It is matter of keeping any response on point, not getting entangled in thoughts of retribution or wallowing in thoughts of recourse. You have been called to one path, and your burden is to stay the course and attend to the path to which your Father has called you, casting off the chaos that thrashes about you.

You may ask, *What about the loss of trust and good will that inevitably results from betrayal?*

In deference to truth, there is no erasing the damage that befalls a relationship with an act of betrayal. An actual fracture has occurred. The point to keep in mind when this happens is the clarity that such a moment brings to the situation. You know the ground you stand upon: You stand in the presence of one who would betray you. In turn, you can build your interior response accordingly. Betrayal ruins relationships; so your relationship is ruined. Now what? Again, the answer is the same: Keep your mind fixed upon the vocation that is before you under God, and the holy graces that attend you will cover the ruination. This is not to suggest that the relationship will be restored—it might be or it might not be. Either way, the only way forward requires an extra measure of grace—grace beyond the natural and the visceral. Just as any restoration that might take place after a betrayal can only be realized by divine intervention, so the ongoing alienation can also only be endured by means of such grace. This kind of grace arises in the cultivation of the virtues. And the virtue of simplicity offers clarity and practicality to even the most troublesome interludes of life's journey.

Francis the Simple

Francis was the embodiment of the virtue of simplicity when, in 1219, he had made a journey to Damietta, Egypt, for the purpose of meeting with the Saracen (Muslim) Sultan, Malik al-Kamil, during the Fifth Crusade.[120]

Historically, this was a complicated moment in the outworking of that crusade, as competing leaders held differing strategies as to how to engage the Saracens, who were holding forth in the region, a critical choke hold to the Holy Land. At the point when Francis arrived at the Crusader camp in Damietta, the Christian forces had successfully taken a strategic tower (in August 1218) under the leadership of the king of Jerusalem, the man named Jean de Brienne, a French knight who'd led the Victory of the Tower. A thirteenth-century Italian Franciscan and historian named Fra Salimbene (1221–1290) wrote an indispensable source for the history of Italy titled the *Cronica*, covering the period between 1168 and 1288. He describes de Brienne as "large, heavy, tall in stature, robust and strong and so expert in the art of war that he was considered another Charlemagne. When in combat he struck here and there with his bludgeon, the Saracens fled as if they had seen the devil or a lion ready to devour them. In his time there was no knight in the world braver than he."[121]

As a result of the Victory of the Tower, the Sultan was ready to concede Jerusalem to the Christians. However, at that moment the Crusader army was under the command of a papal legate, a Cardinal Pelagius, who was described by one historian as a "fanatical Spaniard, fiercely impressed with his own rank." Pelagius possessed catastrophic theories about how to win the war and refused the Sultan's terms. Instead, he demanded the Sultan give up Egypt along with Jerusalem. Thus, when Francis entered the camp, the Cardinal's forces were poised to attack Damietta. According to Francis's biographer, Thomas of Celano, Francis "approached the Christians with salutary warnings, forbidding the war, denouncing the reason for it." But, Thomas adds, "truth turned to ridicule and they hardened their hearts and refused to be guided."[122] Francis took his concerns to the previous commanding officer, Sir Jean, who recognized the wisdom of Francis's words and agreed that they should call for a truce with the Saracens and avoid a great slaughter. But the die had been cast. All pleas for restraint went unheeded. So, as history notes, the Christians went to battle with the Saracens in the siege of Damietta on August 29, 1219, the anniversary of the death of John the Baptist. A massacre ensued. The historian Arnaldo Fortini notes, "The battle was irretrievably lost. The Saracens had reached the Christians' trench. If it had not been for the great valor of the king, Jean, and of the Hospitallers, Templars, and Alemanni, all the Christians would have been killed or taken slaves."[123] Five thousand Christians fell in the battle and a thousand more were taken prisoner.

This was the point at which Francis informed Cardinal Pelagius of his intention to cross enemy lines and seek a meeting with the Sultan. The Cardinal refused to grant permission. Francis went anyway, accompanied by Brother Illuminato, at great personal risk for them both.

Given the complexity of the encounter that unfolded, as I did in my biography of Francis, here I use a multiplicity of sources to cobble together bits to create a picture of how this extraordinary visit unfolded. One source, *Ernoul*,[124] wrote: "When the Saracen sentinels saw them coming they thought that they were messengers or perhaps had come to renounce their faith. They met them, seized them and led them to the Sultan." Thomas of Celano adds, "Although he was ill-treated by many with a hostile spirit and a harsh attitude, Francis was received very graciously by the Sultan." *Ernoul* continues: "When they were brought into his presence, Francis and [Brother] Illuminato greeted him. The Sultan returned their greeting and asked if they wished to become Saracens. . . . They responded that they never would want to become Muslims, but that they had to come to him as messengers on behalf of the Lord God, that he might turn his soul to God. 'If you believe us,' Francis said, 'we will hand over your soul to God because we are telling you in all truth that if you die in the law which you now profess, you will be lost and God will not possess your soul. It is for this reason that we have come.'"

Another source, simply called *Anonymous*, recounts a fascinating moment that highlights the simplicity and clarity Francis brought to this encounter. According to this source, the Sultan wanted to test the faith and fervor that Francis manifested toward the crucified Lord. So he had a beautiful multi-colored carpet spread out on the ground, almost entirely decorated with motifs in the form of crosses. He said to his sages, "If, in coming toward me he walks on the crosses of the carpet, I shall ask him why he insults his Lord. If he refuses to walk on the carpet, I shall ask him why he disdains to approach me." *Anonymous* continued:

"Francis walked across the carpet from one end to the other and came near the Sultan. The Sultan said to him, 'You Christians adore the cross as a special sign of your God. Why then did you not fear to trample underfoot those crosses woven in the rug?' Francis answered, 'This is the cross of bad thieves, the symbol of brigands. We possess the true cross of our Lord.'"[125]

Two other early biographers concluded the story. Julien of Speyer wrote, "With great eloquence he neutralized the arguments of those railing against the Christian faith." Henri d'Avranches concluded, "While he thus teaches the articles of faith with skillful tongue, he impresses sages and kings, nobody dares to harm him."[126]

Francis departed the presence of Malik-al-Kamil after a visit of many days, laden with the supplies as a gift from the Sultan and with the latter's warmest good wishes. Throughout this improbable encounter, Francis kept his intended purpose ever in his mind: to visit the Sultan and try to win him to Christ. Nothing would dissuade or detract him. His purpose was singular, which meant it was driven by the exercise of the virtue of simplicity.

Yet there was another moment during this lengthy trip to Egypt when Francis was called upon yet again to exercise such a virtue.

Revolt

This trip inevitably meant for Francis a prolonged absence from the business of overseeing the Order at home in Umbria. His absence revealed some of his followers' true colors. In the summer of 1220, as Francis departed the Crusader camp in Damietta and before he had begun the long, winding trip back to Assisi, a friar named Stefano arrived from Italy with troubling news. This brother had spent months trying to track down Francis, because he wanted to convey the urgent news that some of the brothers back home had presumed Francis was dead and had taken it upon themselves to change rules and procedures within the Order. The changes involved, among other things, days for fasting and rules about eating meat. There had also been maneuvering about oversight of the Poor Clares. Stefano reported to Francis that his closest companions—people such as Brothers Giles and Leo—were being abused and shunned. Stefano explained that an all-out revolt was underfoot, and it seemed less a rejection of Francis's ideals than a rejection of Francis himself.

Francis's response to the news of this betrayal reflects his exercise of the virtue of simplicity. He had been sitting at the table preparing to eat with his close friend Pietro of Catanii when Stefano arrived with the news. Francis looked at Pietro, recognizing that they were about to eat meat on a day that—according to the revised rules drummed up by the rebels—meat had been forbidden. Francis said, "Lord Pietro, tell me what we ought to do."

Pietro said, "We shall do whatever you want to do, because to you alone belongs the privilege of giving orders."

Francis answered, "Then we shall obey the Holy Gospels and eat what is put before us."

The turmoil and betrayals would continue for Francis once he made his way back to Assisi. Being rejected by his own Order would define the remaining few years of his life. Most of Francis's earliest companions by this time had retreated to hermitages. Francis himself was driven into isolation with only a small core of devoted friends. At points he grew agitated and exasperated and once exclaimed to one of his companions, "Who are these people? They have snatched my religious congregation out of my hands. What more do they want?"

He would often spend nights alone praying in abandoned churches and in deserted places where, wrote one biographer, "with the protection of divine grace, he overcame his soul's many fears and anxieties." Another biographer said that "Francis would make the groves re-echo with his sighs and bedew the ground with his tears." Yet, all accounts of Francis's suffering due to betrayal highlight the great holiness that came out of it. Indeed, these trials did evoke holiness in Francis—but it was a holiness forged in the crucible of rejection and betrayal amid feelings of failure and depression. "Repressing the movements of his nature, he occupied himself with God alone," writes his first biographer, Thomas of Celano. "He often chose solitary places to focus his heart entirely on God." During this season he exercised and upheld his focus: to stay fixed on God and to execute his holy purpose.

What You Hold, Hold

Clare's exercise of the virtue is reflected in a short passage of the second letter she wrote to Agnes of Prague, where she spurred her on to be resolute and immovable in her mission, bending all else to that purpose:

> What you hold, may you hold,
> what you do, do, and never abandon.
> But with swift pace, light step, unswerving feet
> so that even your steps stir up no dust,
> may you go forward securely, joyfully, and swiftly
> on the path of prudent happiness,
> not believing anything, not agreeing with anything
> that would dissuade you from this resolution
> or that would place a stumbling block for you on
> the way,
> so you may offer your vows to the Most High
> in the pursuit of that perfection to which
> the spirit of the Lord has called.[127]

The implication for both Francis and Clare is, when circumstances thrash and disturb, the ballast and clarity of the virtue of simplicity settles the storm and turns the tide. Ponder the clarity the Lord exhibited in the moment of his own betrayal; consider the simplicity with which Francis approached, engaged, and eventually won the heart of the Sultan. Remember the same simplicity with which Francis proceeded in the face of revolt and opposition within his own Order. And reflect upon Clare's simple exhortation: What you do, *do.* In each instance, these holy ones measured the facts of the situation and proceeded to act in accordance with obedience to the holy gospel. They kept going, overthrowing the thrashings of the mind and subduing them under the assertion of virtue. De Sales wrote, "Simplicity is nothing else than an act of pure and simple charity, having only one aim and end, which is to acquire the love of God; and our soul is simple when we have no other aim in all we do or desire."[128] They subverted all other impulses save this aim. They used uncertain moments as a foothold to reach the higher ground of simplicity. This is why St. Francis has said that "holy simplicity confounds the wisdom of the world and the flesh."

In other words, what's big is big, what's little is little. There is a world that is complicated and distorting and there is a place of calm and clarity. There is distinction, in other words, and that distinction is true. There is no falsehood in it. It is discernible and unchanging. Mister Rogers sometimes would ask his television neighbors, *What do you do with the mad that you feel?* Then he would help his viewing audience navigate such angry feelings, inviting children to the Neighborhood, a safe place filled with quiet, simple moments, like feeding the fish. He would sing a song and talk about things like big and little. And in his silent, subtle, and mighty way, he rescued children from a complicated, frenzied, and shallow world that would warp their souls. He showed them, instead, the place where the highest and truest aspects of life are found in that which is deep and simple.

Prayer

That I might bless the Lord
Who conserves all—
Heaven with its countless bright orders,
Land, strand and flood,
That I might search the books all
That would be good for any soul;
At times kneeling to beloved Heaven
At times psalm-singing;
At times contemplating the King of Heaven,
Holy the Chief;
At times at work without compulsion,
This would be delightful;
At times picking kelp from the rocks
At times fishing
At times giving food to the poor
At times in carcair (solitary cell)[129]
—St. Columba, in exile

To Ponder

Have you discerned the singular task or purpose to which the Lord has called you? Is this purpose sufficient to stay the thrashings of tumult and trouble and keep you steady and your gaze fixed in the proper direction?

Has there been an occasion when you have been betrayed? And amid the disorientation of such betrayal, have you been able to exercise the virtue of simplicity and keep your focus on the purpose to which God has called you? Or, as Mister Rogers might ask, *What do you do with the mad that you feel?*

CHAPTER SEVEN
WISDOM

Holy Wisdom confounds Satan and his wicked ways.

Trusting in your inspired words, I shall cry out:
What diversity, Lord, in your creatures!
What wisdom has designed them all!
The beginning is Wisdom and Wisdom is the Beginning
in which you made heaven and earth.[130]
—St. Augustine

If "simplicity aims steadily at acquiring the love of God," as noted by Francis de Sales,[131] then simplicity enables one to keep calm when inwardly vexed and agitated. Such calm and self-control, while fruits of the exercise of all the virtues, are especially evidenced in gaining the ballast of wisdom. This is the last of the four virtues explored in this offering.

When considering the virtue of holy wisdom it seems self-evident that this virtue, of them all, is "won" rather than aspired to. The psalmist says that "Fear of the LORD is where wisdom begins" (111:10). How does the virtue of wisdom arise amid so formidable an aspect of God's being?

By "fear" I don't mean terror; I mean it in the sense of a proper ordering. This can be seen and understood in Francis's seminal theological work, the Canticle of the Creatures. I call the Canticle "theological" despite its being a lyrical song[132] because it expresses a proper ordering of who God is in relation to his creation. Once a proper ordering is landed upon, then all that proceeds thereafter finds its place in keeping with God's holy purpose, and this, in turn, confers wisdom. Francis, near the end of his life, saw this and bequeathed to his brothers and to us all the ability to grasp it through the writing of this song. So take a minute to traverse with me the landscape of God's creation through the eyes of the saint who, at the end of his life, saw it and who bequeathed the wisdom of seeing it.

Francis's initial assertion in the Canticle draws the proper lines and so sets the context for all that follows: *Altissimo*—"Most High." This proclamation marks the opening salvo:

Altissimu onnipotente bon Signore,
Tue so' le laude, la gloria e l'honore
Et onne benedictione.

Ad te solo, Altissimo, se konfàno
Et nullu homo ène dignu te mentouare.

Most high, omnipotent good Lord,
To You all praise, glory, honor, and every blessing.

To You alone, Most High, do these belong,
And no human is worthy to speak Your name.

Francis is asserting that God is "Most High," and everything that follows arises from that fundamental truth. The Italian suffix *issimo* is affixed to a word to convey ultimate force. It is a hurling expression, as if to cast forth a word with greatest strength. There is no comparable vernacular for expressing the strongest possible of terms. By ascribing to God the Italian word *Altissimo* Francis is establishing an immediate sense of proportion. God is foremost, all and everything, and there is nothing on earth or in heaven that rises to his holy position.

Yet in the same stanza Francis adds a disclaimer: "no human is worthy to speak Your name." If, on the one hand, Francis's entire message and purpose has been to point the way toward knowing and loving God, what might he mean in this strophe, where he asserts that no one is worthy even to speak God's name?

Altissimo expressed Francis's recognition of the lowly place where he stood under the mighty merciful hand of God. Such clarity had the effect of causing him (as it would anyone) to fall silent before him. It is the same effect that Job experienced when he was confronted by God, who had asked, "Will the one who disputes with the Almighty correct him? God's instructor must answer him." Job responded only by muttering, "Look, I'm of little worth. What can I answer you? I'll put my hand over my mouth."[133] At the point when Francis wrote the Canticle, he had lived his life and had reckoned with seasons of utter failure. He had failed at knighthood, at commerce, at fighting wars. Yet, from the time when he embraced the leper to the time of the Canticle's writing, the gloom of his early life had undergone a complete transformation. He expressed this transformation in the Canticle's assertion that God is at once high and above all (*Altissimo*), but also near, in keeping with proper proportion. Understood in that way, the Canticle expresses the ways in which God's beauty and nearness ray forth from every aspect of creation. At the end of his life Francis saw heaven's light everywhere, somehow even amid his own failures and weakness.

To understand the power of the Canticle one needs to appreciate the moment in his life when Francis wrote it. Given its lyrical qualities, its tone of delight, and its bursts of celebration, one would be forgiven for assuming he had written it in the prime of his life while strolling along the Umbrian countryside with a spring in his step, the sun on his face, a breeze at his back, and birds playing gleefully about him. Such bliss, one would think, would naturally effervesce and burst forth into song.

Yet the opposite was true. Francis composed the Canticle near the end of his life when his health was spent and he suffered great distress from multiple maladies. He could barely walk, was in constant pain, and was nearly blind due to an eye malady he had contracted while in Egypt. He had been rejected by his own Order and had endured scorn and neglect by younger novices. He was suffering, in other words.

If there had been any consolation for him during this excruciating stretch of time, it had been that when he composed the Canticle, he had taken refuge at San Damiano under the devoted watch care of Clare. (This would be the last time they would see one another.)

His closest companion, Brother Leo, described the occasion:

> Two years before his death, already very sick and suffering especially from his eyes, he was living in a cell made of mats near San Damiano. During his stay at this friary, for fifty days and more, blessed Francis could not bear the light of the sun during the day or the light of the fire at night. His eyes caused him so much pain that he could neither lie down nor sleep.
>
> One night, as he was thinking of all the tribulations he was enduring, he felt sorry for himself and said interiorly, "Lord, help me in my infirmities so that I may have the strength to bear them patiently."[134]

He heard the Lord's response as perceived in his praying: "Be glad and joyful in the midst of your infirmities and tribulations. As of now live in peace as if you were already sharing my kingdom."

> The next morning he said to his companions, "I should be full of joy in my infirmities and tribulations, seek my consolation in the Lord. Therefore, for his glory, for my consolation, and the edification of my neighbor, I wish to compose a new "praises of the Lord" for his creatures. These creatures minister to our needs every day. Without them we could not live. Through them the human race greatly offends the Creator

> [since] every day we fail to appreciate so great a blessing by not praising as we should the Creator and dispenser of all these gifts." He sat down, concentrated a minute, and then cried out: *Altissimu. . . .*[135]

Following that assertion, Francis proceeded in a rapturous eruption celebrating the beauty, utility, and energy of all creation. He opened the song with praise for the glory of "Brother Sun" and carried such praise throughout to include all elements of God's created order.[136]

All praise be Yours, my Lord, through all Your creatures,
And first my lord Brother Sun,
who brings the day; and You give light to us through him.
He is beautiful and radiant with his great splendor,
giving witness of You, most High.[137]

All praise be Yours, my Lord, through Sister Moon and Stars;
In the heavens You have made them, bright
and precious and fair.[138]

All praise be Yours, my Lord, through Brothers Wind and Air,
fair and stormy and all the weather's moods,
by which You give sustenance to all that You have made.[139]

All praise be Yours, my Lord, through Sister Water,
So useful, lowly, precious, and pure.[140]

All praise be Yours, my Lord, through Brother Fire,
Through whom You brighten up the night.
How beautiful he is, how playful!
Full of power and strength.[141]

All praise be Yours, my Lord, through Sister Earth, our mother,
Who feeds us in her sovereignty and produces
various fruits and colored flowers and herbs.[142]

All praise be Yours, my Lord,
through those who grant pardon for love of You
through those who endure sickness and trial.[143]

They are blessed who endure in peace,
By You, Most High,
they will be crowned.[144]

All praise be Yours, my Lord,
through Sister Bodily Death, from whose embrace
no mortal can escape:
woe to those who die in mortal sin.[145]

They are blessed whom you find doing Your holy will!
The second death can do no harm to them.[146]

Praise and bless my Lord,
and give Him thanks,
and serve Him with great humility.[147]

Francis depicts "Brother Sun" as the "*porta significatione*"—the doorway to understanding God. What he means by this he describes elsewhere: "The sun is the most beautiful of all creatures because it is the one which, better than all the others, could be compared to God."[148] I saw the power of the sun and how it is used as a metaphor for God demonstrated in an inexplicable way when I lived in Assisi. The town's buildings are made of pinkish limestone called the *Pietra di Assisi* (stone of Assisi) and on clear days, when the late sun fades in the western horizon, as night approaches there comes a magical moment when the sun's final rays cast a mysterious and iridescent blush over the rose stone face of Assisi's ancient dwellings. In this moment it seems the buildings themselves outshine the light that falls upon them. That is the way the presence of God does its work upon a human heart. When his glory falls upon a heart of stone, the stone itself becomes alive with light.

All other facets of the created world are properly ordered and enlivened by the energy emanating from the sun. So Francis then turns to the moon and stars. They, in their spheres, present the reflection of the sun's light. Francis describes this light as precious and beautiful and clear, using the word "*clarite*," an allusion to Clare's name. God is praised through Sister Moon and all the stars because they are the light-bearers and reflectors of the sun's brilliance.

Then he captures the essence of "wind and air"—that is, all weather conditions, "*onne tempo.*" Weather was very much a part of Francis's everyday existence, whether the air was temperate or the winds bracing. In fact, in a conversation he shared with his close companion Brother Leo, Francis used the condition of the weather as the backdrop for exhibiting "perfect joy." Leo had asked him, *What is true joy?* Francis answered that true joy would be if—when he might come to the gate covered with mud, cold and icy, freezing and exhausted, and, after knocking and calling for a long time—a friar finally comes bringing the hope of entrance and warmth, but then says that he can't enter because the Order has become so important that they no longer need him. Francis said to Leo that true joy would be manifested if, in such a moment, he kept patience and didn't get upset. So God is praised through Brother Wind and all weather, sometimes serene and sometimes fierce, despite the contingencies and inconveniences that may attend it.

Francis celebrates Sister Water in its constant flow, mercy, and cleansing attributes. His image of water is pure, chaste, forceful, and a basic necessity of life. God is praised through Sister Water who nourishes the earth, and who is unstoppable, cleansing, and healing.

Francis refers to Brother Fire as strong, useful, beautiful, playful, and powerful. As a complement to the work of the sun, he says that while "at sunrise every person ought to praise God for having created [the sun] which gives light to our eyes during the day; at evening, when night falls, everyone ought to praise God for that other creature, our Brother Fire, which enables our eyes to see clearly in the darkness. We are all like blind people, and through these two creatures God gives us light. Therefore, for these two creatures and for the others that serve us each day, we ought to praise their glorious Creator in a very special way."[149]

Near the end of his life he was nearly blind because of an eye infection and underwent a brutal treatment of eye cauterization with a searing iron rod and without anesthesia. It involved the doctor placing the rod into the burning coals. When the rod turned red the doctor withdrew it from the fire and readied to apply it to the temples beside Francis's damaged eyes. Francis attempted to look at it but could not tolerate its brightness. But before the procedure, he stopped momentarily, made the motion of the cross over it, and said, "Brother Fire, God has made you beautiful, and strong, and useful. Be courteous with me this hour."[150]

Nearing the completion of his song, Francis turns his thoughts to Sister Earth. God is also praised through Sister Earth, he says, who, nourished by the sun, gives praise to God through gentle assertions, governing all life on the planet, bringing forth fruit and herbs for nourishment and colorful flowers for the pleasure of beauty.

At the song's end, Francis departs from the theme of the elements of natural creation, adding a strophe that relates directly to an ongoing conflict that persisted between two townspeople in Assisi, both his friends, the *podestà* (mayor) and Assisi's Bishop Guido.[151] The latter had been and continued to be a major force in the beginnings and ongoing development of the Friars Minor.

The mayor had been a strong supporter of Francis, and his daughter had joined Clare at San Damiano. So, near the end of his life and hearing of their conflict, Francis added this strophe: "All praise be Yours, my Lord, through those who grant pardon for love of You." He asked a few of his brothers to go to town and sing the Canticle in the presence of both men.[152] They went and said to both of them, "Despite his sufferings, brother Francis has composed the 'Praises of the Lord,' to praise God and for the edification of his neighbor. He asks you to listen with great devotion."

Both had known of Francis's suffering, and when the brothers sang, the words of the Canticle seared their hearts and moved them to make peace with one another. So God is praised when peace reigns between neighbors, for to live in peace requires meekness and charity, the mark of humility and true humanity.

The strophe highlighting Sister Death was also a late addition. Francis added it when he was informed by his physician that he would soon leave this world. In that moment, he embraced his mortality, crying out, "Welcome, Sister Death!" He saw even mortality as being numbered among the gracious gifts that God renders to and through his creation. Even Sister Death praises God, he says: No person can escape it. They are blessed who, embracing it, have come to find God's "most holy will."

Francis himself exhibited this glorious vision of holy death as he himself was in the process of dying. As his descent into death bore down, he had told his brothers, "When you see me *in extremis* lay me down naked on the earth and leave me there for as long as it takes to walk a leisurely mile." By early morning October 3, 1226, that moment came. Death closed in. Francis's eyes were shut, his face in a grimace of pain. His breathing became labored. At nightfall, when the languor of death descended, he asked his brothers to lay him down on the ground. There Francis wept as his brothers surrounded him singing the Canticle. It was as if he himself were singing his last song, and more, that he himself were part of the song. The Italian historian Arnaldo Fortini said that in the Canticle, "All the lost relationships of Eden call out." At his moment of death, in the singing of the Canticle, all his losses had been righted, all that had been lost was found. "I call upon you, O Lord," he said. "Come quickly to me."

Mortality itself renders praise to God. They are blessed who are found in "Your Most Holy will" and who serve God with great humility.

Set Your Heart on Heaven

The reader may wonder how Francis's recitation of praises for the attributes of creation relates to the virtue of wisdom. The answer is simply that there is deep wisdom hidden in the Canticle, and apprehending it captures the aspirations of the virtues. "God . . . knows which gifts to give to the day and which to the night," writes St. Augustine, "so that you too may know and for you there may be lights in the firmament of heaven. But this cannot be unless you set your heart on heaven." He concludes:

> [Y]ou must go where he leads and abash the strong. Go where he leads, you welcome messengers, . . . shine over all the earth and let the day, radiant in the sunlight, utter the word of wisdom to the day: let the night, gleaming in the light of the moon, impart the word of knowledge to the night. The moon and the stars shine by night, but the night does not darken them, for it is they that give it light.[153]

The Canticle's wisdom lies not so much in the specificity with which Francis celebrates creation's various components—anyone with eyes can see that Sister Earth produces flowers and herbs and that Brother Fire is playful and robust. These features are self-evident. The wisdom that is seen in the Canticle is realized in appreciating that, at the time of his composing it, Francis himself *didn't* actually have eyes with which to see such things; he had become blind and was in great physical distress. Yet, despite not seeing and being physically distressed, Francis perceived the glory that lay hidden behind every element of creation. He perceived that each of these elements carried their own little bits of that glory, and that the granularity of each respective operation was part of the divine symphony of the expression of that glory. Even in his blindness and physical suffering, he saw it. And he did not simply see it, but he rose up in song to celebrate it and himself became part of the song.

It comes back to proportionality, the proper ordering of all things. Once God is given his rightful place as highest and greatest, as *Altissimo,* all that flows out from his great glory reflects "little glories" of their own. It takes great wisdom to understand God's great glory and to see all of the little glories that remit it back to him. Once you can see that, then afflictions, sorrow, struggles, and all things that keep us pinned to earth can be measured in proper proportion.

Such Holy Wisdom enlightens human repose and settles the cacophony of false narratives, human betrayals, and all the chaos that afflicts a soul. It casts its gaze and turns a listening ear to the glorious symphony being played out at all times and everywhere in God's creation, unified in the single purpose of celebrating the *Altissimo* of God. Wisdom lends eyes to recognize it and ears to hear it. More than that, wisdom shows us the way to find our place in the symphony. George MacDonald said, "The sun is shining golden above me; the sea lies blue beneath his gaze; the same world sends its growing things up to the sun, and its flying things into the air which I have breathed from my infancy; but I know the outspread splendor [to be] a passing show, and that at any moment it may, like the drop-scene of a stage, be lifted to reveal more wonderful things."[154] Holy wisdom lifts that curtain.

Gaining wisdom is both the beginning and the end of the holy reordering of the soul. It is the beginning in that, at the very onset of the journey one is obliged to assert *Altissimo,* to give God his place and to bring proper order and proportion. Wisdom is also the end point in that, so ordered, the vows and virtues create the interior environment where, just as the sun works its energy over the earth, dross is burned away from a troubled soul and God's nature begins to emerge.

Inevitably, there will be hard, sad times when despite best efforts and true conviction, a soul passes through dark valleys. In such times it seems as if eyes cannot see, and the holy exertions take on the feel of an echo calling out amid a cavernous void. There are times when God's inexplicable movements leave you lost, flailing, and blind.

Wisdom lends ballast during such disorienting passages. Remember the harmony and simplicity of the operations of the sun, how it illuminates and animates all things. When the storms come, wisdom stays the troubled soul as a captain of a heaving ship on a roiling sea rights his ship.

"Get wisdom," the Proverb says. "Though it cost you all you have, get understanding. Cherish her, and she will honor you. She will give you a garland to grace your head and present you with a glorious crown."[155]

Prayer

Look upon us, O Lord,
and let all the darkness of our souls
vanish before the beams of Your brightness.
Fill us with holy love,
and open to us the treasures of Your wisdom.
All our desire is known unto You,
therefore perfect what You have begun,
and what Your Spirit has awakened us to ask in prayer.
We seek Your face.
Turn Your face to us and show us Your glory.
Then shall our longing be satisfied,
and our peace shall be perfect.[156]
—St. Augustine

To Ponder

Do you agree with the notion that the virtue of wisdom arises from seeing things in proper proportion? In what way, as you see it, does making the assertion *Altissimo* when speaking of God bring things into such proportion?

Have you found your place in God's symphony? If so, has finding it lent you wisdom? How does such wisdom show itself in your life?

CONCLUSION

The singers and the dancers will say,
"All my springs are in you."
—Psalm 87:7 (ESV)

As I conclude this exploration, I have pondered an element of living the Franciscan Way that has not yet been mentioned and does not fall under the categories of vows and virtues. That is the implied significance of "church" as part of the fundamental apparatus of growing in holiness. I used the term loosely because there are a variety of ecclesial expressions that claim to capture the essence of what it means to belong to Christ. When I pray on my bed late at night during those bewitching hours when thoughts sometimes turn to primal lament, when questions about all you've lived for and manifested in your life come into high relief—when things of God seem as if they don't make sense; I have heard myself utter to our Savior—*So it all comes down to this? An aging woman lying in her bed at night praying with her prayer beads repeating the prayer "Jesus, Son of David, have mercy on me"? This is what it all comes down to?* I ponder the vaulted ceilings of great cathedrals or the monstrance of the mass lifted high, I recall services of praise in contemporary church traditions where not the monstrance but the open palms of the people are lifted in praise. I consider, what does any of this have to do with this prophet from Galilee who summoned fishermen and anyone else who would listen, to "follow" him? Did he lead them into churches with vaulted ceilings or auditoriums with worship bands? He led them to lonely places where they stood to the death by the testimony of their friend who changed the landscape of his times and their lives and who is still changing the landscape of all times and our lives.

Where does "church" fit into this picture? This is a sore subject for me since I was married to a pastor. And when our crisis had reached its nadir and I turned to the church leadership for help and intervention, they abandoned me in deference to my husband's dismissals of my plea. Thereafter I stopped believing in the "biblical" church. This made it very difficult to find a path forward within that context, and I have flailed.

I pressed on. I found some worship settings that authentically moved me and brought a degree of healing. I've also experienced worship settings that have caused me to roll my eyes. (Part of the instability of my post-divorce life has been moving around a lot and thus finding myself in diverse worship settings.) The experience of a variety of church expressions across varied traditions has led me to the sense that each iteration of devotion carried something of true light, even if only as a shard of light, while, at the same time, none of them carried all of the light.

Shards of light are the best possible means for fallen humans to experience a touch of God's glory. So it could be said that it is part of God's design that "church," of itself, is imperfect and inadequate. It cannot be the actual reflection of God's glory, because who of us could bear it? It is a mere sliver, a hint of it, for that is as much as we humans could handle. As Annie Dillard put it: "Does anyone have the foggiest idea what sort of power we so blithely invoke? Or, as I suspect, does no one believe a word of it? The churches are children playing on the floor with their chemistry sets, mixing up a batch of TNT to kill a Sunday morning. It is madness to wear ladies' straw hats and velvet hats to church; we should all be wearing crash helmets. Ushers should issue life preservers and signal flares; they should lash us to our pews."[157]

You may be asking, *Are you saying, then, that to live the Franciscan Way, you need to go to church?* When I consider the answer to the question I think foremost of Francis himself, who lived an itinerant life and so was frequently absent from a settled church setting. He was much loved by Assisi's Bishop Guido and equally so by the renowned Bishop Ugolino who would later become Pope Gregory IX. So Francis was intimately connected to the operations of the church and was devoted to the rhythms and manifestations of worship. He regularly prayed the offices and partook of the Eucharist. His closest friend and traveling companion, Brother Leo, was an ordained priest (an anomaly for the Friars Minor) who carried with him a satchel with a chalice and paten so that wherever he and Francis would go, they would have the apparatus and elements needed to partake of the mass. So, while it could be said that Francis wasn't a "church-goer," the accoutrements of strict devotion were never far from him.

Yet beyond the habits of Francis himself, the Franciscan Way requires us to consider the church issue through the proper lens. We are commanded to love the Lord our God with all our heart, soul, mind and strength,[158] which means that we are compelled, through obedience, to ask ourselves if we are doing that as we make our way along the Franciscan path. Are we giving God the honor he is due?

In addition to pondering the place of church out of obedience, the Franciscan Way also compels us to consider the operations of God through the coming of his son, Jesus, whom Francis followed, and who he bade his own brothers and sisters to follow. Beyond the renunciations and mortifications and above the exercise of virtues, there is another layer of operation that, if we are following Jesus, we are called to. I heard the rector of an Episcopal church put it this way: "The choir director has a piece of music for which he needs a choir to sing so as to be heard around the world. In your singing you can follow him."

Church can be seen as the apparatus, an arbiter, to negotiate the path between the clay feet of humanity and the glory of God. You go through personal confessions, sing hymns, exercise the rhythms of prayers with a granularity that might not always carry immediate meaning. Maybe you didn't "sin" that week, so you don't feel meaning behind the rote confession, "We bewail our manifold sins which we from time to time most grievously have committed." Yet the exercise of the readings and rituals works upon a soul in a way that is perhaps not unlike the effect that befell people who were confronted with the person of Jesus when he walked the earth. The granularity of these movements carries the effect of an astringent that cleanses rough edges, heals wounds, and refreshes one's being. Where else but in church might one hear the words of comfort, "Thou art the same Lord whose property is always to have mercy"? It might not be witnessing Jesus walking on the water or feeding multitudes. But it carries an impact nonetheless. As Frederica Mathewes-Green says it, "We can't understand it, but fortunately, we don't have to. What we receive each Sunday in dumb incomprehension is what we are receiving, through prayer, in a lifetime of submission to God's will and his leading. We are gradually being healed, restored, 'deified,' enabled to bear the presence of God, just as we receive that presence in a material way in Communion."[159]

Regardless of tradition, in any case, the Franciscan Way supersedes denominations. It can find a foothold in any church context in the same way the mail of armor covers any warrior going to battle regardless of which side he is on.

Concluding Thoughts

I didn't live my life aspiring to live the Franciscan Way. I carried differing ambitions. When a version of the faith system I had appropriated collapsed, as noted earlier, the Franciscan Way *found me* unbidden. It entered through the back door, and, in time, it overtook my life. I clamored against it for a time, that is, until at some imperceivable point, it turned me inside out and I looked up and saw grace. It had become a holy, hidden, mysterious gift.

When I ponder my hopes behind sharing this story and consider why I wrote this book, I have come to see that my purpose was not driven by a desire to reroute whatever path you may find yourself upon. This is not what one would call a "how-to" manual for growing in Franciscan spirituality. Far from it. I am the last person who could presume to wear the mantle of a Franciscan guide. Yet I do write as one whose life and belief system were shipwrecked and who found an improbable rescue through an endearing eccentric saint. He met me in my wreckage, took me by the hand (and at times by the scruff of the neck), and led me along a higher path. My life was worth saving, in other words, though the terms were stark and felt at times untenable. Step by step Francis led me along, introduced me to his friends, and rekindled the remnant of elements of authentic faith that had survived the storm. The way I worship, the work I do, the relationships I build are as unique and as individual as God's calling upon my life. But they are forever transformed because they have been infused with the balm of the exercises I've noted herein, the balm of living the Franciscan Way.

It has been the exercises that have carried me through, because, when life does its work, when (borrowing again from Fred Buechner) it "slays us all," the emotive side of the faith journey fails. You don't always "feel" God's presence. You lie in your bed praying prayers with prayer beads and can't always perceive that anyone is listening. As Mother Teresa experienced it, "all is darkness." This is where the exercises of vows and virtues establish a landing spot for an otherwise confused, sometimes faltering faith journey. Keep going, they prod. Do this; keep doing it—you'll find your way through.

The Franciscan Way, through an inversion process of relinquishments (vows) and aspirations (virtues) will carry you to your intended purpose: finding God, seeing at long last that he is near, true, loving, and on your side. He made you, after all, and desires to see you bloom as the flower you are destined to be. So these ingredients in combination with your specific and unique gifting, vocation, and aspirations will work the magic of the garden on your soul, and you will rise as a fully formed flower, unique to you and reflective of the best that God intends for you.

When I pray the Jesus Prayer—"Jesus, son of David, have mercy on me"—the Spirit prompts me to recall how the story of that cry ends. The blind man Bartimaeus had called out that prayer, even against the dismissive and stifling efforts of Jesus's own disciples to rebuke him at the time. Ignoring the background clamor, Jesus turned to the persistent blind man and asked, "What do you want me to do?" The blind man responded, *I want to see!* And so, in keeping with his merciful and generous nature, Jesus granted the blind man's plea.

Praying the Jesus Prayer certainly has its place. But it is important to remember that when Bartimaeus repeatedly cried out that plea, Jesus asked him what he wanted him to do, and then, once the request was stated, Jesus equally desired so to deliver. So, just as he instructed the blind man, he bids us, too, to speak what we want him to do. Then, once it is done, he bids us to get up, go forth, and get on with our (now healed) lives that God destined and desires for each of us.

So, in answer to my own question above—*Does it all come down to lying in bed at night praying with prayer beads repeating the prayer, "Jesus, Son of David, have mercy on me"?*—the answer is both no and yes. The answer is yes in the sense that there is a place in Christian devotion for repetitive praying. Such utterances can assist us to "pray without ceasing" and are part of operation of the Holy Spirit that helps us to pray "with sighs too deep for words." The answer is also no—the Christian life does not simply come down to praying the Jesus Prayer with prayer beads on one's bed. At some point, as Jesus responded to Bartimaeus, he bids us to see and to walk. There is work to be done and *that*, ultimately, is your purpose and your destiny. The intended result of living the Franciscan Way is not to turn your world upside down, as Francis's world was and as were the worlds of those who followed him. The Franciscan Way, more, is a summons to shift your gaze from false distractions, craven appetites, and self-interest. It's a call to lift your eyes to a higher mountain, to experience the clarity of humility, the fleetness of simplicity, the freedom of charity, and the assurances of wisdom. The Franciscan Way points to a life that is lived with well-ordered constraints and that sees all things in proper proportion—the holiness of creation and our place in it—abiding in dignity and resting in absolute trust in a loving, intimate, and ever-near God.

Back to the Garden

Looking back upon the landscape of the topics explored in this short volume, I'm seeing lofty themes like the benefits of prayer, the graces of spiritual direction, the rewards of interior resolve, and the help of church. Each in its own way helps to mark the path that leads along the Franciscan Way.

Yet, when the moments come when such lofty themes lose their sheen and feel elusive, I always return to the garden. The most meaningful act that keeps me going along the winding road of faith is to plant a seed. Once that small act has been realized, it sets in motion the universe of operations that affect miracles, new beginnings, and expanded possibilities. So go to your garden center and supply yourself with an emergency spiritual healing kit to have on hand when the hard moments come. Purchase a plastic seeding tray and high-quality, nutrient-dense soil, and think about a type of flower or herb or other living thing you would like to enjoy, and purchase a pack of seeds. Then, when that day comes when you have lost hope or faith or feel abandoned or unable to find your way, pull out the seeding tray and pack it with soil, poke a center hole in each plug and drop in a seed. Gently cover the seed with a light top layer of soil, water it, and place it in the sun. The miracle will start to happen. It will be invisible at first, so it will require patience—but it is patience that is tempered with hope. Remember to be vigilant! The miracle requires your partnership; growth will happen only through the attendance of your vigilance. Remember to water it gently and keep the tray warm and receiving plenty of light. If you do your part, the power of all that is good in this world will do its appropriate work. You will have joined forces with the Author of Life and Light and co-created a miracle. And the picture you will see when the seedling starts to assert itself is the picture of your own soul rising from the dirt into new life. This is the picture of the fruit of plodding along the path of the Franciscan Way. It takes time, even as the silent growth of a growing garden cannot be rushed. But the fruits of it are true, pure, and hopeful.

All that is required of you is to woo him humbly in prayer
and at once he will help you.
Call upon him then, and let us see how you will get on.
He is always most willing and is only waiting for you.
So what are you going to do?
How will you move him?[160]

ACKNOWLEDGMENTS

I wish to thank my publisher, Paraclete Press, and the excellent people there, most notably, Bob Edmonson, who took me on and brought me along and helped me navigate this project. I am especially grateful for the wise counsel of Lillian Miao, who rendered compassionate and timely guidance at a point when I needed it. I am likewise grateful for and indebted to my readers Brian Payne and Kate Harrison Belz, who devotedly slogged through the early draft offering valuable feedback. I owe a special debt of gratitude and offer my sincere and humble thanks to my guide, advocate, editor, and friend, Jeff Crosby, without whose efforts on many levels, from beginning to end, this project would not have been realized. At many turns when my own assurances faltered, he steadied me and continued to assert his belief in me as a writer and also in this effort.

As a final note, I would like to acknowledge the many loving and praying friends who knew that the season of the writing of this book dovetailed with a period of great personal trial. These trusted godly people lifted me and carried me on the wings of their prayers, and I am grateful to them and to the Lord, who heard them.

APPENDIX

WENDY'S RULE

Assisi, 2005

1.

Through Christ and the gift of his Spirit,
give thanks at all times and in all places and in all things.

2.

What you hold, hold
What you do, do—and never abandon—
with a swift pace, a light step,
unswerving feet so that you do not stir up dust;
Go forward securely, joyfully, swiftly in prudent happiness;
do not believe anything or agree with anything
that would turn you from your resolution
or put up a stumbling block along the way.
(St. Clare)

3.

Entrust to the Truth everything the Truth has given you,
and nothing will be lost.
(St. Augustine)

4.

Whoever proves a hindrance or heartache to you, reckon it a grace;
love those who do these things to you,
and do not wish something else from them
and do not wish that they be better Christians.
(St. Francis)

5.

If there is anyone who may have sinned even to the utmost degree,
let them not—having looked into your eyes—come away without mercy.
And if they are not looking for mercy, ask in your own way if they desire mercy.
Then, even if they should continue to sin before your eyes a thousand times more,
love them all the more, that you may draw them to the Lord.
And always be merciful.
(St. Francis)

GLOSSARY OF TERMS

Abbot/Abbess: A friar or sister who is in charge of a particular monastery.

Basilica/Cathedral: *Basilica* was originally used to describe a Roman public building; the term has evolved to refer to a large and important church that has been given special ceremonial rites by the pope while retaining an aspect of public accessibility for architectural, artistic, or ecclesiastical purposes. A cathedral, on the other hand, is a Christian church that contains the seat of a bishop. It is intended for worship and serves as the bishop's seat, thus as the central church of a diocese.

Bull (Papal bull): In Roman Catholicism, a papal bull is an official papal letter or document. The name is derived from the lead seal (bulla) traditionally affixed to such documents. Since the twelfth century it has designated a letter from the pope carrying a bulla that shows the heads of the apostles Peter and Paul on one side and the pope's signature on the other. (Britannica)

Curia: The Roman Curia, taken from the Latin word that means "court," is the administrative counsel of the central governing body of the Roman Catholic Church. It is comprised of the pope and cardinals.

Divine Offices: Saint Benedict of Nursia (c. 480–543) is credited with creating a structure organization for the liturgy of offering prayers at various points of the day, including morning, the third hour, the sixth, the ninth, the evening, and at "cock-crowing." The eight "Divine Hours," called the Divine Offices, are known by the following names:

Matins (during the night or predawn hours of the morning)
Lauds (at dawn)
Prime (First Hour = 6 a.m.)
Terce (Third Hour = 9 a.m.)
Sext (Sixth Hour = 12 noon)
None (Ninth Hour = 3 p.m.)
Vespers ("at the lighting of the lamps"—evening)
Compline (before retiring)

General Chapter: The gathering of all elected representatives of the Order from all provinces to discuss business, make decisions, share fellowship, and set a course for the future.

Hagiography: An important literary genre in the early Christian church, providing historical information as well as inspirational stories and legends. (See below).

Legend: A book of record of the deeds of a saint; not intended to be a biography in the strict sense.

Mendicant (Latin *mendicare*, "to beg"): A member of a religious Order in the Roman Catholic church who takes a vow of poverty renouncing personal and communal property. The term evolved to describe those in the penitential movement who went from place to place to preach.

Minister General: The head of the Order within each respective branch of the Franciscans (Conventual, Observant, Capuchin).

Order of Friars Minor

Observant (OFM): The Observant branch strives to uphold the simple lifestyle modeled by Francis. They live in hermitages. Their tunics are brown. They shave.

Conventual (OFM Conv): "The Conventuals," in the Middle Ages, was a generic designation for Franciscans who lived in a stable house (*conventus* in Latin) and not in caves and hermitages. This branch encourages education and the building of universities. Their tunics are gray or black. They wear blue jeans outside the convent.

Capuchin (OFM Cap): The Capuchin friars, which evolved in the sixteenth century, sought to return to and uphold the primitive way of life in solitude and penance as practiced by the founder of the Order. They wear a brown tunic and usually have long beards.

Order of Saint Clare of Assisi or "Clares" (OSC): The "Poor Clares," as they are also sometimes called, is a Franciscan Order founded by Clare (as the Order of Poor Ladies) to establish communities of women who want to embrace the penitential life as embraced by Francis.

Third Order Franciscans (TOF): Also called the SFO—Secular Franciscan Order—was created in 1221 by Francis to accommodate brothers and sisters of the penitential movement who wished to live by the order's convictions but were prevented from joining because of marriage or other ties.

Penitent: In the twelfth and thirteenth centuries religious penitents were those who put themselves in the service of God by attaching themselves in service to a particular church or monastery. In all cases, the emphasis of the penance was to practice justice and mercy, to trust in God, to be of pure heart and intent, to have a zeal for Christ and the Scripture, and to be open to God's grace and inspiration. Most of the participants had little or no formal theological training, and many developed heretical beliefs. [Wiki]

Rule: The governing document of a religious order.

Sacro Convento: The friary, or living quarters, in Assisi connected to the Basilica of San Francesco.

Saracens: Another name for the Arab empire (Muslim) under the rule of the Umayyad and Abbadis dynasties.

Templars: Also known as Knights Templars, they were a medieval Christian military Order prominent in the Crusades from the early 1100s until the early 1300s.

Tonsure: In the Roman Catholic Church the "first tonsure" (a symbolic cutting of hair about the size of a coin leaving a bare spot toward the back of the head) was, in medieval times, the rite of qualifying someone for the civil benefits then enjoyed by clerics, primarily the privilege to preach.

ABBREVIATIONS

Material taken from *Francis of Assisi, Early Documents* and *Clare of Assisi, Early Documents* are denoted in the notes as FA:ED and CA:ED, respectively.

1LAg The First Letter to Blessed Agnes of Prague (1234)
2LAg The Second Letter to Blessed Agnes of Prague (1235)
3LAg The Third Letter to Blessed Agnes of Prague (1238)
4LAg The Fourth Letter to Blessed Agnes of Prague (1253)
FLCl The Form of Life (1253)
TestCl The Testament (1247–1253)
BlCl The Blessing
PrPov The Privilege of Poverty of Pope Gregory IX (1228)
FLInn The Form of Life provided by Pope Innocent IV (1247)
PC The Acts of the Process of Canonization (1253)
VL The Versified Legend (1254–1255)
BC The Bull of Canonization (1254)
LCl The Legend of Saint Clare (1254–1255)

Franciscan Biographical Writings
1C The First Witness of Thomas of Celano (1228)
2C The Second Witness of Thomas of Celano (1245–1247)
AP The Witness of the "Anonymous of Perugia" (1240–1241)
L3C The Legend of the Three Companions (1241–1247)
AC The Assisi Compilation (1244–1260)
LJS The Life of Saint Francis, Julian of Speyr
MP Mirror of Perfection
LegMaj Major Legend of Bonaventure
VL The Versified Life of Saint Francis by Henri d'Avranches

NOTES

INTRODUCTION

1 1 Corinthians 6:19–20.

2 The sixteenth and seventeenth centuries saw the Franciscans play a critical role in the Counter-Reformation, frequently suffering martyrdom in England, the Netherlands, and Germany. During the nineteenth century their numbers diminished because of effects of the Enlightenment and political upheaval in Spain, Italy, and France. At the same time the Order was flourishing in North America, and varying branches of Franciscans today rank among modern Catholicism's most prolific and influential male Orders. See Wendy Murray, *A Mended and Broken Heart* (Basic Books, 2012), 180.

3 In the Middle Ages this was a generic designation for Franciscans who lived in a stable house (*conventus* in Latin) and not in caves and hermitages.

4 The female Order, founded by Saint Clare, is the "Second Order," while the male Order originating with Francis was simply the "First Order," known also as the "Friars Minor." There are countless examples of laypeople who adopted the Third Order who would go on to live out Franciscan principles and influence their world.

One such example is that of St. Margaret of Cortona (1247–1297), who was born in Tuscany, Italy, the only child of a working-class family. She lost her mother at age seven and had a poor relationship with her stepmother. Margaret was spoiled, willful, reckless, and beautiful, and at the age of seventeen she left her father's house in the night and became the mistress of a young nobleman. She lived with him in his family castle for nine years and bore him a son, but he did not marry her due to her lower social class. One day he did not return home from a journey, and his hound came back to the castle alone. The dog led Margaret into the nearby wood where she discovered her lover brutally murdered. This shook her to her core. Her eyes were opened to the sinfulness of her way of life, and she became deeply repentant. She left his family castle with her son and sought out the Franciscan friars for spiritual direction. She then reformed her life through prayer, penance, and self-discipline, eventually joining the Third Order of St. Francis, living in poverty and showing charity toward the poor.

St. Margaret of Cortona is the patron saint of the homeless, reformed prostitutes, midwives, single laywomen, the mentally ill, and the falsely accused. Her feast day is February 22. (Adapted from the Catholic Encyclopedia, https://www.newadvent.org/cathen/09653b.htm)

5 Regis J. Armstrong, J. A. Wayne Hellmann, and William J. Short, eds., *Francis of Assisi Early Documents* (hereafter denoted as 5FA:ED), vol. 3 (New City Press, 2001), 469.

6 Basic Books, 2008, 2012. Hereafter my book will be denoted in the notes as *Mended.*

7 From a collect in the *Book of Common Prayer* (Oxford University Press, 1789).

Part One
FINDING FRANCIS

8 See my book *On Broken Legs* (NavPress, 2004), 150.

9 "Anatomy of a Divorce," Pat Conroy, *The Atlantic*, November 1, 1978.

10 Francis de Sales, *Finding God Wherever You Are* (New City Press, 1993), 29.

11 Ephesians 4:26.

12 Colossians 3:16.

13 Ephesians 5:28.

14 *On Broken Legs,* 153.

15 2 Corinthians 5:17.

16 Francis de Sales, *The Art of Loving God* (Sophia Institute Press, 1998), 93.

WHO WAS FRANCIS?

17 Arnoldo Fortini, *Francis of Assisi*, trans. Helen Moak (Crossroad, 1992), 99. Taken from *Nova Vita di San Francesco* (Tipografia Porziuncula, 1959).

18 This is discussed in great detail in *Mended,* 41–54.

19 *FA:ED*, Henri d'Avranches, *The Versified Life of Saint Francis,* First Book, 150, 170.

20 *Mended*, 41–45.

21 I came across five different years for Clare's birth in a variety of sources. It must be added, however, that determining dates of birth in the Middle Ages is tenuous.

22 "Saint Clare," Paschal Robinson, OSF, from *Franciscan Essays* by Paul Sabatier and others (Aberdeen University Press, 1912), 35.

23 Frederick of Barbarossa predated Francis by a generation. He lived in the fortress above Assisi called La Rocca. He saw it as his mission to assert forcefully the Emperor's power over the ever-strengthening Papacy. To this end, Barbarossa established Roman laws and a legal constitution, which, given the chaos of the age, had been alien concepts. Moreover, because of Pope Gregory VII's decree forbidding bishops to be vassals of the state, Emperor Barbarossa established a network of dukes to maintain local order in their stead. However, Barbarossa's attempt to impose the "rule of law" was not altogether embraced by his dukes, who preferred autonomous rule over their respective dominions. Barbarossa thus added yet another arm of power to consolidate his authority, the *ministerialia*—former military men. He hoped these would prove serviceable and more loyal than the unruly dukes. This new order of armed champions became the defining model of military prowess of the age—noble knighthood. So the stage was set that would define the backdrop of the lives of Francis and Clare: land-owning, uppity, and brutish dukes attempting to control servant peoples (serfs) while knights-in-arms rendered fearless service to the Emperor. Cf. *Mended*, 7.

24 Fortini/Moak, *Francis of Assisi*, 208.

25 *Mended,* 50.

26 *FA:ED,* Vol 1, *Testament of Saint Francis* (1999), 124.

27 *FA:ED,* Vol III, d'Avranches, *Versified Life,* 440.

28 *Mended,* 45.

29 *CA:ED,* "Testament of Saint Clare," 60–61.

30 *Mended,* 109–122.

Part Two
VOWS

INTRODUCTION TO THE VOWS

31 *FA:ED,* Vol. 1, *The Writings of Francis of Assisi, The Earlier Rule,* 75.

32 1 Peter 4:1.

33 *Omnibus of the Sources for the Life of St. Francis, Vol. 1* (hereafter cited as *Omnibus*), ed. Marion A. Habig; trans. Raphael Brown, Benen Fahy, Placid Hermann, Paul Oligny, Nest de Robeck, Leo Sherley-Price (Franciscan Press, 1991), 31.

34 *Omnibus*, 57. An easy way to distinguish the Franciscan friars from other religious orders is their signature three-knotted rope tied about the waist of their tunics; the three knots signify the three vows.

35 *FA:ED*, Vol. III, *Mirror of Perfection* 24, 275.

CHAPTER ONE
POVERTY

36 Francis de Sales, *Letters of Spiritual Direction* (Paulist Press, 1988), 98.

37 Matthew 19:21.

38 Thomas of Celano mentions an earlier follower named John about whom little is known.

39 Matthew 19:21; Luke 9:3, 23.

40 *Omnibus II, Legend of the Three Companions*, 942.

41 Mother Teresa, *Come Be My Light* (Doubleday Religion, 2007), 165.

42 Mother Teresa, *Come Be My Light*, 167.

43 Mother Teresa, *Come Be My Light*, 111.

44 The First Letter to Blessed Agnes of Prague in *Clare of Assisi, Early Documents, The Lady* (hereafter cited *CA:ED*), trans. Regis J. Armstrong, OFM Cap (New City Press, 2006), 45–46.

45 The circumstances of this catastrophic circumstance are not known.

46 *The Book of Divine Consolation of the Blessed Angela of Foligno*, trans. from Italian by Mary G. Steegmann, introduction by Algar Thorold (Duffied & Co., 1909).

47 *The Complete Poetry & Selected Prose of John Donne*, Charles M. Coffin, ed. (The Modern Library, 1994), 474–75.

48 Fortini/Moak, *Francis of Assisi*, 659, n. 92.

CHAPTER TWO
CHASTITY

49 Catechism of the Catholic Church, Second Edition, 2337.

50 Augustine, *Confessions* (Penguin Books, 1961), 164.

51 *FA:ED*, Vol. 2, *Remembrance of the Desire of a Soul*, Celano, 325.

52 Saint Benedict of Nursia (c. 480–543) is credited with creating a structure of organization for the liturgy of offering prayers at various points of the day, including morning, at the third hour, the sixth, the ninth, the evening, and at "cock-crowing." The eight "Divine Hours," called the Offices, are known by the following names: Matins (during the night or pre-dawn hours of the morning); Lauds (at Dawn); Prime (First Hour = 6 a.m.); Terce (Third Hour = 9 a.m.); Sext (Sixth Hour = 12 noon); None (Ninth Hour = 3 p.m.); Vespers ("at the lighting of the lamps"—evening); Compline (before retiring).

53 2 Corinthians 12:10.

54 Galatians 6:17.

55 G. K. Chesterton, *Orthodoxy* (Image/Doubleday), 93.

56 I discuss this concept at length in my book *Clare of Assisi, Gentle Warrior* (San Damiano Books/Paraclete Press, 2020), 123–125.

57 The following highlights come from the writings of the Third Order Franciscan Angela of Foligno, in *The Book of Divine Consolation of the Blessed Angela of Foligno.*

58 *Divine Consolation,* Chapter XXXIV, "Of the Properties of Lovers."

59 *Divine Consolation*, XXXIV.

60 Matthew 13:45–46.

61 John 1:11.

62 C. S. Lewis, ed., *George MacDonald, 365 Readings* (Collier Books/ MacMillan, 1947), 24.

CHAPTER THREE
OBEDIENCE

63 Francis de Sales, *Introduction to the Devout Life* (Vintage Books, 2002), 10.

64 de Sales, *Introduction to the Devout Life*, 8.

65 For more detail about this episode, see *Mended*, 127–132.

66 A. Valerio, "Women in the 'Societas Christiana' : 10th-12th

centuries." *TD* 33:1 (Spring, 1986), 156.

67 *CA:ED, PC*, I, 6, 146.

68 Francis de Sales, *Letters of Spiritual Direction* (Paulist Press, 1988), 109.

69 Peter Kreeft, *Prayer for Beginners* (Ignatius Press, 2000), 15.

70 Kreeft, *Prayer for Beginners*, 16.

71 Kreeft, *Prayer for Beginners*, 16.

72 Kreeft, *Prayer for Beginners*, 18.

73 Francis de Sales, *The Art of Loving* God, 98.

74 *Saint Augustine's Prayer Book*, Rev. Loren Gavitt, ed. (Holy Cross Publications, 1967), 236.

75 Thomas Merton, *Spiritual Direction and Meditation* (Liturgical Press, 1960).

76 Merton, *Spiritual Direction and Meditation*, 16, 17.

77 Merton, *Spiritual Direction and Meditation*, 34.

78 de Sales, *Introduction to the Devout Life*, 10.

79 de Sales, *Introduction to the Devout Life*, 10.

80 This personal rule can be found in the appendix, page 145.

81 de Sales, *The Art of Loving God*, 43.

82 *Writings of St. Francis*, Ignatius Brady, OFM, trans. (Edizioni Porziuncola, 2002), 39.

Part Three VIRTUES

INTRODUCTION TO THE VIRTUES

83 1 Peter 1:13, 15.

84 Thomas à Kempis, *The Imitation of Christ*, Betty I. Knott, trans. (Fontana Books, 1963), 64.

85 *Writings of St. Francis,* 39.

86 de Sales, *Introduction to the Devout Life*, 91.

CHAPTER FOUR HUMILITY

87 de Sales, *Introduction to the Devout Life*, 96

88 *Omnibus II, LPer,* 991–92.
89 *Omnibus I,* Bonaventure, *Major Life,* 675.
90 *FA:ED,* vol. II, 338.
91 *Omnibus I,* Bonaventure, *Major Life,* 679.
92 *Omnibus II, Little Flowers,* 10, 1322.
93 *Mended,* 81–84.
94 *Omnibus II, Little Flowers,* 25, 1356–59.
95 *Gentle Warrior,* 44–45.
96 *Gentle Warrior,* 44–45.
97 *FLCl* 3; *CA:ED,* 114.
98 de Sales, *Letters of Spiritual Direction,* 158.
99 de Sales, *Art of Loving God,* 30–31.
100 Frederica Mathewes-Green, *Welcome to the Orthodox Church* (Paraclete Press, 2022), 80.
101 Mathewes-Green, *Welcome to the Orthodox Church,* 80.
102 de Sales, *Introduction to the Devout Life,* 5–6.

CHAPTER FIVE
CHARITY

103 de Sales, *The Art of Loving God,* 29.
104 de Sales, *The Art of Loving God,* 34.
105 de Sales, *The Art of Loving God,* 36.
106 de Sales, *The Art of Loving God,* 34.
107 de Sales, *Finding God Wherever You Are,* 29.
108 The word Paul uses here is *agapē* _(ἀγάπη), a word generally unknown to writers outside of thc New Testament. The King James Version, cited above, denotes the word as "charity," while most other translations use the English word "love." The term ἀγάπη _(*agapē*) connotes a breadth and depth beyond the scope suggested by the English word "love." It springs from a sacred honor or respect, exerted as a decision of will and from self-denying and compassionate devotion. In the context of this exploration, I have opted to highlight the translation of *agape* as it is used the KJV.
109 Some historians conjecture it was written to Peter Catanii. Others assert Francis wrote the letter to Elias. The author is of the mind

that the letter was written to the former.
110 *FA:ED:* Vol. 1, 97.
111 *Omnibus II, Mirror of Perfection* 38, 1163.
112 She is said to have had "the gift of tears."
113 The details of these hardships are outlined in my book *Clare of Assisi, Gentle Warrior.*
114 This is Arnoldo Fortini's translation of the vision described by the Eleventh Witness, Sister Benvenuto, *Life*, 365. See *CA:ED, 1*82.
115 *The Cloud of Unknowing* (Harper San Francsico,1981), 18.
116 John Henry Newman; this quote came from the devotional *Magnificat* for Monday, October 9, 2024, 13.
117 de Sales, *Introduction to the Devout Life*, 85 (alternative translation).
118 https://www.catholic.org/prayers/prayer.php?p=3082, accessed January 3, 2025.

CHAPTER SIX
SIMPLICITY

119 Recounted in my book *Day of Reckoning* (Brazos Press, 2000).
120 This fascinating event is explored at length in my book *Mended*, 109–122.
121 Fortini/Moak, *Francis of Assisi*, 408 ff.
122 *Omnibus II, Celano Second Life*, 30, 388.
123 Fortini/Moak, *Francis of Assisi*, 408 ff.
124 The thirteenth-century chronicler named Ernoul wrote what is widely considered the most accurate of the several attempts to narrate the Crusades as a sequel to William of Tyre's twelfth-century narratives. Ernoul's document is called *The Chronicle of Ernoul* (1227–1229). These documents are found in *Francis of Assisi, the Early Documents*. Fortini includes extensive notes on primary source material relating to this episode (pp. 635–639).
125 He is referring to a relic.
126 See *Mended*, 117–120, n. 14.
127 *CA:ED, 2LAg*, 48.
128 de Sales, *Art of Loving God*, 105.
129 Columcille fecit. *Lyra Celtica*, c. 1894.

CHAPTER SEVEN WISDOM

130 Augustine, *Confessions,* 261.

131 de Sales, *Art of Loving God*, 112.

132 In fact, it is the first such composition in vernacular Italian, and it inspired Dante himself in the writing of his *Divine Comedy.*

133 Job 40:2–4.

134 *Omnibus II, Legend of Perugia* 43, 1020.

135 *Omnibus II, Legend of Perugia* 43, 1021.

136 Interestingly, there is no mention of animals.

137 Laudato sie, mi' Signore, cum tucte le Tue creature, spetialmente messor lo frate Sole, lo qual è iorno, et allumini noi per lui. Et ellu è bellu e radiante cum grande splendore, de Te, Altissimo, porta significatione.

138 Laudato si, mi Signore, per sora Luna e le stelle, in celu l'ài formate clarite et pretiose et belle.

139 Laudato si, mi Signore, per frate Uento et per aere et nubilo et sereno et onne tempo, per lo quale a le Tue creature dài sustentamento.

140 Laudato si, mi Signore, per sor'Acqua, la quale è multo utile et humile et pretiosa et casta.

141 Laudato si, mi Signore, per frate Focu, per lo quale ennallumini la nocte, et ello è bello et iocundo et robustoso et forte.

142 Laudato si, mi Signore, per sora nostra matre Terra, la quale ne sustenta et gouerna, et produce diuersi fructi con coloriti flor et herba.

143 Laudato si, mi Signore, per quelli ke perdonano per lo Tuo amore, et sostengono infirmitate et tribulatione.

144 Beati quelli ke 'l sosterrano in pace, ka da te, Altissimo, sirano incoronati.

145 Laudato si, mi Signore, per sora nostra Morte corporale, da la quale nullu homo uiuente pò skappare: guai a cquelli ke morrano ne le peccata mortali.

146 Beati quelli ke trouarà ne le Tue sanctissime uoluntati, ka la morte secunda no 'l farrà male.

147 Laudate et benedicete mi Signore, et rengratiate et seruiateli cum grande humilitate.

148 *Omnibus II, Legend of Perugia* 43, 1022.
149 *Omnibus II, Legend of Perugia* 43, 133.
150 *Omnibus II, Legend of Perugia* 48, 1026. The attending doctor was amazed by the grace and fortitude with which Francis endured so brutal a procedure. Alas, in the end, it did nothing to improve his condition and only increased his suffering.
151 Fortini/Moak, 577.
152 Fortini/Moak, 579.
153 Augustine, *Confessions,* 327.
154 George MacDonald, *Phantastes* (Eerdmans, 2000), 218.
155 Proverbs 4:7–9, NRSVue.
156 *Prayers of the Early Church,* ed. J. Manning Potts (The Upper Room, 1953), n.p. (Public domain in the U.S.)

CONCLUSION

157 Annie Dillard, *Teaching a Stone to Talk: Expeditions and Encounters* (Harper & Row, 1982), 40–41.
158 Matthew 22:37ff and Mark 12:30.
159 Mathewes-Green, *Welcome to the Orthodox Church*, 77.
160 *The Cloud of Unknowing*, 13.

ABOUT PARACLETE PRESS

Paraclete Press is the publishing arm of the Cape Cod Benedictine community, the Community of Jesus. Presenting a full expression of Christian belief and practice, we reflect the ecumenical charism of the Community and its dedication to sacred music, the fine arts, and the written word.

Learn more about us at our website:
www.paracletepress.com
or phone us toll-free at 1.800.451.5006

SCAN
TO
READ
MORE

YOU MAY ALSO ENJOY: